The Saint John's Bible and Its Tradition

The Saint John's Bible and Its Tradition

Illuminating Beauty in the Twenty-First Century

EDITED BY

Jack R. Baker

Jeffrey Bilbro

Daniel Train

PICKWICK *Publications* · Eugene, Oregon

THE SAINT JOHN'S BIBLE AND ITS TRADITION
Illuminating Beauty in the Twenty-First Century

Pickwick Publications
An Imprint of Wipf and Stock Publishers
199 W. 8th Ave., Suite 3
Eugene, OR 97401

www.wipfandstock.com

PAPERBACK ISBN: 978-1-5326-1838-3
HARDCOVER ISBN: 978-1-4982-4392-6
EBOOK ISBN: 978-1-4982-4391-9

Cataloguing-in-Publication data:

Names: Baker, Jack R., editor. | Bilbro, Jeffrey, editor. | Train, Daniel, editor.

Title: The Saint John's Bible and its tradition : illuminating beauty in the twenty-first century. | edited by Jack R. Baker, Jeffrey Bilbro, and Daniel Train.

Description: Eugene, OR: Pickwick Publications, 2018. | Includes bibliographical references and index.

Identifiers: ISBN 978-1-5326-1838-3 (paperback). | ISBN 978-1-4982-4392-6 (hardcover). | ISBN 978-1-4982-4391-9 (ebook).

Subjects: LCSH: Saint John's Bible. | Bible—Illustrations. | Illumination of books and manuscripts. | Beauty.

Classification: N72 R4 S15 2018 (print). | N72 (ebook).

Manufactured in the U.S.A.   09/20/18

To our children, who we hope will fall in love
with the beauty of the Word.

Contents

Figures

Figure 1. *Creation,* Donald Jackson with contributions from Chris Tomlin, Copyright 2003, *The Saint John's Bible,* Saint John's University, Collegeville, Minnesota, USA. Used by permission. All rights reserved.

Figure 2. *Ten Commandments,* Thomas Ingmire, Copyright 2002, *The Saint John's Bible,* Saint John's University, Collegeville, Minnesota, USA. Used by permission. All rights reserved.

Figure 3. *Judges Anthology,* Donald Jackson, Copyright 2010, *The Saint John's Bible,* Saint John's University, Collegeville, Minnesota, USA. Used by permission. All rights reserved.

Figure 4. *Jacob's Ladder,* Donald Jackson with contributions from Chris Tomlin, Copyright 2002, *The Saint John's Bible,* Saint John's University, Collegeville, Minnesota, USA. Used by permission. All rights reserved.

Figure 5. *Bee Error Treatment,* Chris Tomlin; scribe: Sally Mae Joseph, Copyright 2006, *The Saint John's Bible,* Saint John's University, Collegeville, Minnesota USA. Used by permission. All rights reserved.

Figure 6. *Transfiguration,* Donald Jackson with contributions from Aidan Hart, Copyright 2002, *The Saint John's Bible,* Saint John's University, Collegeville, Minnesota, USA. Used by permission. All rights reserved.

Contributors

Paul N. Anderson serves as Professor of Biblical and Quaker Studies at George Fox University and as Extraordinary Professor of Religion at the North West University of Potchefstroom, South Africa. Author of over two hundred published essays and author or editor of over a dozen books, his books include *Following Jesus, From Crisis to Christ, The Christology of the Fourth Gospel, The Fourth Gospel and the Quest for Jesus,* and *The Riddles of the Fourth Gospel.*

Jack R. Baker is Associate Professor of English at Spring Arbor University where he teaches literature and liberal arts courses. He makes his home in Spring Arbor, Michigan, with his wife Kelly and their three children, Owen, Silvia, and Griffin. He is also an amateur writing-shed builder.

Gretchen Batcheller currently lives in Malibu, California, where she is an Associate Professor of Studio Art at Pepperdine University. Gretchen's work can be found in both public and private collections both in the United States and abroad. She has also participated in numerous regional, national, and international exhibitions including shows in Los Angeles, Philadelphia, and New York, as well as Eisenstadt, Austria; Rome, Italy; and Istanbul, Turkey.

Jeffrey Bilbro is an Associate Professor of English at Spring Arbor University in southern Michigan. He grew up in the mountainous state of Washington and earned his B.A. in Writing and Literature from George Fox University in Oregon and his Ph.D. in English from Baylor University. His books include *Loving God's Wildness: The Christian Roots of Ecological Ethics in American Literature, Wendell Berry and Higher Education: Cultivating*

Virtues of Place (written with Jack Baker), and *Virtues of Renewal: Wendell Berry's Sustainable Forms.*

David Lyle Jeffrey (Ph.D. Princeton; Fellow of the Royal Society of Canada) is Distinguished Professor of Literature and Humanities at Baylor University. He is also Professor Emeritus of English Literature at the University of Ottawa, Guest Professor at Peking University (Beijing). He is the author of *People of the Book: Christian Identity and Literary Culture* (1996), and, with Greg Maillet, *Christianity and Literature: a Philosophical Approach to Literary Criticism* (2011) and a theological commentary on *Luke* for the Brazos Press (2012). His most recent book is *In the Beauty of Holiness: Art and the Bible in Western Culture* (2017).

Robert Moore-Jumonville serves Spring Arbor University as Professor of Christian Spirituality in the Department of Theology. He has written books on American biblical criticism and G. K. Chesterton. An elder in the United Methodist Church for thirty years, he has served as senior pastor for three churches (in Illinois, Indiana, and Michigan).

Matthew A. Rothaus Moser (Ph.D. Baylor University) is lecturer in theology at Loyola University Maryland, where he teaches courses on Augustine, Dante, theology and literature, and the Christian imagination. He is the author of *Love Itself Is Understanding: Hans Urs von Balthasar's Theology of the Saints* (2016) and the forthcoming *Dante and the Poetic Practice of Theology.*

Jane Kelley Rodeheffer is a philosopher who currently holds the Fletcher Jones Chair of Great Books at Pepperdine University in California. Professor Rodeheffer received degrees from Boston College, Harvard, and Vanderbilt. She has published a range of articles in philosophy, literature, and great books, and she is the coeditor of three collections of essays. She is currently at work on a project involving the use of narrative Icons in the work of Dostoevsky. A potter and calligrapher in the Asian tradition, she served as artist in residence at the Saint John's University Pottery in Collegeville, Minnesota, for the summer of 2016.

Sue Sorensen lives in Winnipeg, where she teaches English at Canadian Mennonite University. Her latest book (2014) is *The Collar: Reading Christian Ministry in Fiction, Television, and Film.* She is the author of a novel, *A*

Large Harmonium (2011), and the editor of *West of Eden: Essays on Canadi-an Prairie Literature* (2008). She is a published poet and has done academic work on topics ranging from A. S. Byatt, Henry James, Ian McEwan, and Guy Vanderhaeghe to detective fiction, children's books, rock lyricists, and the filmmaking of Neil Young.

Daniel Train is the Assistant Director of the Duke Initiatives in Theology and the Arts (DITA) in Durham, NC. He directs the Certificate in Theol-ogy and the Arts for graduate students at Duke Divinity, coordinates DITA programming, and teaches courses at the intersection of Theology and Lit-erature. He has published essays on a variety of subjects, including Bede's biblical commentaries, Ernest Hemingway, and Irish poet Eavan Boland. His current book project is titled *Naming Beauty: Flannery O'Connor and the Hermeneutics of Peace.*

Acknowledgments

THIS PROJECT WAS BIRTHED from a regional gathering of the Conference on Christianity and Literature at Spring Arbor University in February 2016. Spring Arbor University was hosting a Heritage Edition of *The Saint John's Bible*, and this formed the inspiration for the conference theme. After hearing many excellent presentations on *The Saint John's Bible*, we began talking about a way to make these contributions more broadly available. We invited contributions from other scholars who had been unable to attend the conference, and this volume gathers the results of these conversations. We are especially indebted to Jim Triggs, Father Michael Patella, and the community of Saint John's University for their support and encouragement throughout our time with the Bible. We are also grateful for Emily Spencer, Morgan Caroland, and Julia Mayer who helped us to format these essays and compile the index.

Jack Baker would like to thank Spring Arbor University for supporting our work with *The Saint John's Bible*, especially Bill Zeller and Harold Dunckel, who crafted a splendid wooden case to house the Heritage Edition of *The Gospel and Acts*. I am ever thankful for the love of Kelly, Owen, Silvia, and Griffin.

Jeff Bilbro is grateful for the churches and student groups with whom I had opportunities to share *The Saint John's Bible*; their questions and comments deepened my own understanding of its beauty. And I am deeply grateful for the love I share with Melissa and Hannah.

Dan Train is immensely grateful to Jeremy Begbie, Director of the Duke Initiatives in Theology and the Arts (DITA), who has given me the opportunity to be part of such an exciting initiative at Duke Divinity. Professor Begbie's scholarship and inspiring vision for a rigorously theological engagement with the arts has played an absolutely vital role in the development of this field, and I consider it a great honor to be working alongside someone whose life and work I so deeply admire. Many thanks also are due to Richard Hays, who not only made it possible for me to join DITA but has been one of the strongest advocates of the Theology and Arts program at Duke. Likewise, the many talented graduate students I have worked with at Duke have not only taught me to see more deeply and think more clearly, but they have been unbelievably gracious despite my many shortcomings and unfailingly enthusiastic in their support. I also wish to thank David L. Jeffrey whose teaching and writing informs nearly every page of this volume. Finally, I wish to thank my wife, Hillary, and two daughters whose presence gives me life.

1

Introduction

IN AN AGE OF e-books and screens, it may seem rather antiquated if not downright antediluvian to create a handwritten, illuminated Bible. The Benedictine monks at Saint John's Abbey and University, however, determined to produce such a Bible for the twenty-first century, a Bible that would use traditional methods and materials while engaging contemporary questions and concerns. Given the remarkable riches of this admittedly idiosyncratic work, this collection of essays examines how *The Saint John's Bible* fits within a history of the Bible as a book, focusing especially on how its haptic and aesthetic qualities may be particularly important in a digital age marked by fragmentation and disagreement.

In an era that largely assumes the physical form of a book is a mere vessel for disseminating information, *The Saint John's Bible* foregrounds the importance of a book's tactile and visual qualities as both a response to and an aid for rightly understanding sacred Scriptures. Like their premodern exemplars, the creators of *The Saint John's Bible* understood that the physical *form* of the text would itself exert a certain kind of *form*ation in the hermeneutical and theological imaginations of its audience. For example, opening a Bible app on an iPad conditions us to practice the same reading techniques we have learned from reading other texts on screens: we tend to skim quickly, extract information, and move on when we become distracted.[1]

In contrast, opening the pages of this handwritten, beautifully illuminated Bible fosters a different set of reading practices. As Rowan Williams, the former Archbishop of Canterbury, explains about *The Saint John's Bible*, "We tend to read greedily and hastily, as we do so many other things; this

---

1. For an analysis of how people tend to read on screens, see Baron, *Words Onscreen*.

beautiful text . . . offers an insight into that lost skill of patient and prayerful reading."[2] The remarkable, almost obsessive attention to detail, craftsmanship, and quality of materials testify to the prayerful vision behind this project, a vision that is clearly motivated by concerns other than profit and easy consumption. Indeed, as this collection seeks to show, the physical, haptic experience of reading *The Saint John's Bible* is itself an invitation for readers to meditate deeply on the beauty of God's self-revelation in his word.

For all its interest in preserving the virtually extinct craft of manuscript illumination, however, *The Saint John's Bible* is emphatically not driven by a naïve nostalgia or technophobia. Rather, at the heart of the project is an abiding appreciation for the way certain modern construals of the dialogic relationship between word and image have created both an opportunity and a need for a book like *The Saint John's Bible*. Like their contemporaries who live in an image-saturated, hyperlinked, and emojified culture where meaning and power are increasingly inextricable from the media in which they are embedded, the artists of this remarkable text have embraced the possibility (and responsibilities) of manifesting the Gospel's ever-newness to an audience which recognizes that letters and words are not merely static symbols. For the team of artists and scholars behind *The Saint John's Bible*, our non-linear reading practices and growing expectation that texts will be hyperlinked shares at least some affinity with the medieval practices of internalizing the Sacred texts in one's memory so as to hear the whole of Scripture within each individual passage. As in medieval manuscript illuminations, repeated images and visual themes throughout *The Saint John's Bible* provide crucial hermeneutical guides for (hyper)linking the two Testaments and reading the whole of the Scriptures at one time.

Similarly, the images in *The Saint John's Bible* draw on centuries of tradition and on contemporary, technological concerns. For instance, the opening page in Matthew depicts Jesus' family tree in the form of a Jewish menorah, a symbol that goes back to the Pentateuch; yet spiraling through the branches of the candlestick are the double-helix pattern of DNA. Jesus is the divine Messiah, and in the mystery of the incarnation he is also part of the Jewish human family. Another example can be found in the illumination of the *Luke Anthology*, which combines images from many of the parables and stories that are unique to Luke (see Figure 8). Donald Jackson was working on this page on September 11, 2001, and he placed the twin towers alongside the father welcoming home the prodigal

2. Saint John's University, "A Year with *The Saint John's Bible.*"

son. The image suggests how the forgiveness the father practices in this story continues to guide Christians today as we seek to offer a word of reconciliation and renewal.

Moreover, in order to make this beautiful book accessible to more people, Donald Jackson directed the production of *The Saint John's Bible Heritage Edition*. Creating these 299 high-quality reproductions pushed the technical capacities of modern printing. Uncoated cotton paper was needed to replicate the look and feel of vellum, but uncoated cotton absorbs ink too readily, leading to bleeding and poor color resolution. A new printing technique was used that employs ultraviolet rays to dry the ink almost immediately after it hits the paper. The gold and silver are then applied to the illuminations with a precision embosser, and many of them are hand finished. Thus no two copies of the Heritage Edition are identical, and each copy recreates the three-dimensional texture of the original manuscript.

The Saint John's Bible, then, draws on the resources of revelation and tradition as it engages with contemporary forms, subjects, and materials in order to prompt a reawakening of the Christian tradition and imagination. Yet, it must be acknowledged, the modern technologies on which *The Saint John's Bible* relies for both its imagery and its reproduction have also spawned forms of persuasion that are less prayerful, to put it mildly. The contemporary world bombards its inhabitants with slogans and ads and memes, all clamoring for attention. These forms of persuasion aim to seduce their subjects into buying particular products, manipulate them into voting for a candidate, or even terrorize them into submission; they view language and image as means of dividing, coercing, and gaining power.

But *The Saint John's Bible* is emphatically not marshalling word and image in this way, either for easy, unreflective consumption or for political gain. How might we, then, distinguish aesthetic and physical forms whose beauty issues an invitation to prayer and transformation, from those forms whose aim is to manipulate and coerce? With this question in mind, the essays in this collection both draw on and aim to recover a theological account of beauty in order to better elucidate and distinguish the redemptive, prayerful power of *The Saint John's Bible*. In doing so, we seek not only to restore the language of beauty within the Christian tradition, but also to offer a re-imagining and re-membering of "power" and "persuasion" as the Gospel's proclamation of a peace that passes all understanding and promise of a transformation which makes all things new.

Embedded in the Christian tradition is a keen sense of beauty's power to transform those whom it encounters. Whether it be the shepherds' wonder at the angel choir's announcement, or the disciples' slow growth while listening to Jesus' parables, or John's dazed worship when encountering the glorified Son of Man, or Dante's sanctification through studying purgatorial art, there are countless examples of the deep change that beauty can effect. Testimonies to beauty's power are not limited to the Christian faith. The poet Rilke, while a heterodox Christian at best, famously describes art's force in his poem "Archaic Torso of Apollo." At the end of the poem, this ancient statue suddenly shifts from being a static object of observation and instead examines the viewer with transformative power: "for here there is no place / that does not see you. You must change your life."[3]

Thus, the essays in this collection draw on the rich theological resources that describe beauty's role in divine revelation and in God's redemption of his people. In his "Letter to Artists," Pope Saint John Paul II describes art's "unique capacity to take one or other facet of the [Gospel] message and translate it into colours, shapes and sounds which nourish the intuition of those who look or listen." He goes on to articulate the way that art can make divine mystery perceptible: "In order to communicate the message entrusted to her by Christ, the Church needs art. Art must make perceptible, and as far as possible attractive, the world of the spirit, of the invisible, of God. It must therefore translate into meaningful terms that which is in itself ineffable."[4]

For everyone, then, believers or not, genuine works of art inspired by Scripture reflect the unfathomable mystery which engulfs and inhabits the world. The beauty of *The Saint John's Bible* has moved Christians and non-Christians in the years since its completion. John Paul II speaks to this unifying quality of the beautiful when he claims that "even in situations where culture and the Church are far apart, art remains a kind of bridge to religious experience." Art can function as a bridge because beauty uniquely is able to cross boundaries: between secular and religious, human and divine, finite and infinite. Libraries around the world have exhibited *The Saint John's Bible* or purchased Heritage Editions, and its calligraphy and illuminations have caused many to see the biblical text anew. *The Saint John's Bible* is a work of art that, according to Pope Saint John Paul II's definition, has the ability to translate or, quite literally,

3. Rilke, *Selected Poems of Rainer Maria Rilke*, 147.

4. Paul, "Letter to Artists."

transform the biblical text "without emptying the message itself of its transcendent value and its aura of mystery."[5]

As Alasdair MacIntyre argues in works such as *After Virtue* and *Whose Justice? Which Rationality?*, rational discourse becomes strained when it takes place across incommensurable traditions, and the result is the shrill public discourse we have today.[6] Beauty offers a way forward in such a context because, as David Bentley Hart demonstrates, Christian beauty is a mode of peaceful persuasion, one that invites rather than berates, attracts rather than compels.[7] At the end of *After Virtue*, MacIntyre famously calls for a new St. Benedict, someone who will live the gospel in a credible manner before a skeptical world. Perhaps *The Saint John's Bible* can teach us how to answer MacIntyre's call by making the Kingdom of God perceptible through its aesthetic form. Such an artistic witness stands as a peaceful mode of persuasion, one that invites participation in divine beauty. It is in this way that a Church attuned to the various embodiments of beauty might be a transformative witness in a fragmented culture. A greater understanding and appreciation of the transformative power of beauty can aid the church in tuning human souls to divine harmony, to participating in the Kingdom of God.

Chapter Summaries

In the opening essay, David Lyle Jeffrey draws attention to a central paradox of Christian worship: no human response is adequate to God's glory, and yet when we encounter his glory, we can't help but attempt to respond with the best praise we can muster. One of the forms this response has historically taken has been the creation of beautiful art that gratefully points toward the holy presence of God. The practice of lavishly illuminating and decorating biblical manuscripts is part of this broader tradition, and such beauty emphasized the Scripture's value and holiness. While the Protestant emphasis on making the Bible accessible through vernacular translation and the printing press had many good results, one unfortunate consequence was the interruption of this practice. In turning to the ways in which *The Saint John's Bible* recovers this sense of Scriptural beauty, Jeffrey emphasizes how God's word reconfigures our aesthetic sense. Thus we

5. Ibid.

6. MacIntyre, *After Virtue*; Macintyre, *Whose Justice?*

7. Hart, *The Beauty of the Infinite*.

can learn to recognize Christ's crucifixion, which would seem to be ugly and deformed, as deeply beautiful, a recognition aided by *The Saint John's Bible's* golden illumination of this event. Contemplating this image, Jeffrey reminds us that Christ's beauty reforms our merely human standards and invites us to embody his love in our own lives.

Jeffrey notes that Augustine played a key role in helping the church articulate and understand the strange, unsettling beauty of the cross, and Matthew Moser begins his essay with the distaste Augustine experienced when first reading the Bible. Moser argues that we should expect the Scriptures to disrupt our aesthetic sensibilities, and he suggests that the ancient practice of *lectio divina* can aid in the slow, painful work of reordering our tastes and affections. Through a meditation on the frontispiece of Genesis, Moser progresses through the four stages of *lectio divina—lectio, meditatio, oratio,* and *contemplatio—*in order to demonstrate the transformation that such prayerful, ruminant reading can effect in our minds and affections. The illuminations in *The Saint John's Bible* can help us encounter the strange beauty of divine revelation in a way that reorders our very selves so that we can become more fully transparent to the God whose image we bear.

Our deep restlessness, our hurry and busyness and distraction, can cause us to miss such encounters with God. In his essay, Robert Moore-Jumonville shows how the depictions of Christ in *The Saint John's Bible* often portray him as obscured, but they also hold out hope that if we seek him patiently and prayerfully, we will find ourselves illuminated by his presence. *The Saint John's Bible's* size and format, along with its beautiful art, prompt us to slow down, to attend, to wait. Beauty, like the search for God and the process of spiritual growth, cannot be rushed. In this way, the beauty of *The Saint John's Bible* might act as "a salve" that could heal our blind eyes so that, like the disciples on the road to Emmaus, we can see Jesus sitting next to us.

These three opening essays put *The Saint John's Bible* in a historical and theological context that elucidates how its beauty can help us better read the Scriptures. The following essays build off these insights in examining particular facets of *The Saint John's Bible's* aesthetic. Jack Baker draws our attention to the manuscript's errata as reminders of our human fallibility and God's power to redeem and beautify our mistakes. The essay—which is auto biographical, academic, and pastoral—considers the world of manuscript margins and the creatures that populate their open fields. Errata inevitably enter the landscapes of manuscript pages, making their homes both within the text itself and the images, regardless of the care taken to produce a polished book. No matter where they appear on the page, scribes have always had to cultivate creative remedies for their mistakes, which is something we lose in modern print culture. The slowness manuscript pages invite us to practice, then, is formative, instructing us that though we're not always able to erase our errors, we can learn creatively to live with them. Such hope encourages us to flourish despite our missteps—a hope that is at once temporal and eternal.

Many of the depictions of Jesus in *The Saint John's Bible* are decentered and indeterminate, and Sue Sorensen puts these portrayals in conversation with Victorian illustrations by Jacques Tissot, Harold Copping, and William Holman Hunt. While these Victorian artists may be seen as sentimental now, Sorensen shows how their works in fact introduce mystery in their representations of Jesus; through this "reticence," they provoke meditation and can serve as an aid to spiritual growth. *The Saint John's Bible* extends these methods in its own illuminations, and Sorensen finds clarifying continuities between these Victorian illustrators and the work of Donald Jackson and his team. Even a "mere glance" at such illuminations can lead to contemplation and inspiration and cause us to see the person of Jesus anew.

Thomas Ingmire's illuminations in *The Saint John's Bible* image Jesus not through decentered or reticent portrayals, but through the very words of Scripture. Dan Train examines several of these illuminations, arguing that Ingmire reveals the way God's covenant with his people, in both the Old and New Testaments, is enacted through his words: God is the "I AM who I AM," the one who speaks the Ten Commandments, and most profoundly the Word who becomes flesh. Ingmire helps us to experience the way that God's words become visible, manifesting not only in the life of Christ, but also in the ongoing life of Christ's body, the church.

In keeping with this corporate emphasis, Jeffrey Bilbro's essay draws attention to the ways that *The Saint John's Bible* personalizes the Word of God without reducing it to a sentimental or consumerist commodity. Medieval manuscripts sought to achieve this goal by depicting the patron in some of the illuminations or decorating the Bible in the aesthetic style of the local culture. Such an endeavor becomes harder after the printing press begins to make books as fungible, impersonal products. The modern printing industry now makes Bibles that meet every conceivable consumerist niche: the Green Bible, the Duck Dynasty Commander Bible, the Busy Dad's Bible. *The Saint John's Bible*, however, recovers the medieval sense of God's revelation as a personal word without succumbing to the consumerist temptations of our contemporary culture. The Bible is a word to us personally, but not to us individually; it does not accommodate its message to our preconceived desires and expectations, rather, it accommodates us to its revelation.

Paul Anderson further explores how *The Saint John's Bible* brings traditional biblical wisdom to bear on contemporary concerns. By featuring women in its illuminations and presenting figures and patterns from cultures beyond Europe and North America, the artwork endeavors to present a global and inclusive perspective on important issues. Further, the illuminations address particularly painful situations within recent years, from the Holocaust, to the bombing of Iraqi fugitives in the first Gulf War, to the reminder of the Twin Towers of 9/11. When considering the meanings of the biblical texts alongside the contributions of the artists, we get a sense of the ways the biblical text speaks powerfully to today's pressing needs—guiding our consciences and understandings to see how the light of Christ might yet still be at work in this thick night.

The book concludes with a very practical essay that describes an ongoing collaboration between students in a Great Books Colloquium and those in a Painting and Drawing course at Pepperdine University. Inspired by the process through which the illuminations in *The Saint John's Bible* were created, Jane Kelley Rodeheffer and Gretchen Batcheller worked to recreate this with students studying Dante's *Divine Comedy* and Milton's *Paradise Lost*. By reading—*lectio*—and ruminating—*meditatio*—on the texts, Great Books students were able to offer their insights into the themes, language, and events to the Art students, who then used their expertise to translate the information into a visual context. Like the theologians and artists who collaborated on *The Saint John's Bible*, humanities and art students were thus able to enter into a centuries old tradition of interpreting and illustrating the *Inferno* and *Paradise Lost*. Ideally, this example will inspire other teachers and communities to find ways of responding to the aesthetic call of *The Saint John's Bible* and so participate in the beauty of God's scriptural revelation.

Bibliography

Baron, Naomi S. *Words Onscreen: The Fate of Reading in a Digital World.* New York: Oxford University Press, 2015.

Hart, David Bentley. *The Beauty of the Infinite: The Aesthetics of Christian Truth*. Grand Rapids: Eerdmans, 2004.

John Paul II, Pope. "Letter to Artists." EWTN, 1999. http://www.ewtn.com/library/papaldoc/jp2artis.htm.

MacIntyre, Alasdair. *After Virtue: A Study in Moral Theory*. 2nd ed. Notre Dame: University of Notre Dame Press, 1984.

———. *Whose Justice? Which Rationality?* Notre Dame: University of Notre Dame Press, 1989.

Rilke, Rainer Maria. *Selected Poems of Rainer Maria Rilke*. Translated by Robert Bly. New York: Harper & Row, 1981.

Saint John's University. "A Year with *The Saint John's Bible*." 2014. https://www.saintjohnsbible.org/promotions/PDF/YearWithTheSaintJohnsBible_2015.pdf/.

2

Beauty in the Bible and the Beauty of Holiness

David Lyle Jeffrey

"Can any praise be worthy of the Lord's majesty?"[1] With this rhetorical question of the Psalmist Augustine begins his *Confessions*, historically the most influential Christian reflection on the growth of the intellectual and spiritual life outside the Bible itself.[2] Stripped of its context, the question becomes effectively, "What gesture of ours will do to honor divine glory?—and the answer is obviously "nothing." But there is, of course, a context; the Book of the Psalms from beginning to end is just what its Hebrew name avers. It is *Tehellim*, praises, poetry to be sung weekly in worship of the Holy One of Israel. Context thus provides us with an inferential question that equally requires an answer: "Shall we then be silent?" Here too the answer must obviously be "no." After all, it is only the wicked who remain silent.[3] The Psalmist everywhere is saying, in effect, "Let the redeemed of the Lord say so!"

> You have turned for me my mourning into dancing; you have put off my sackcloth and clothed me with joy, so that my soul may praise you and not be silent. O Lord my God, I will give thanks to you forever.[4]

1. Psalm 145; cf. 18:3.
2. Augustine, *Confessions* 1.1.
3. 1 Samuel 2:9.
4. Psalm 30:11–12.

This is the premise and context in which the rhetorical question of Psalm 145 invites a strong response; it is likewise, of course, the very reason for Augustine's testimony of praise in his *Confessions*.

So the issue is not whether praise should be offered to God. Nor is it simply a matter of trying to figure out what sort of praise would be excellent enough so as to avoid offering something inappropriate, though that remains a matter for thoughtful reflection since the story of Cain and Abel. The point is simply this: that in consideration of the holiness and glory of the eternal God, omnipotent, omniscient, and beyond all imagination quintessence of the good, nothing which springs from a fallen human imagination can hope to be strictly speaking worthy. Yet the believer is nevertheless called to worship, "to give Him thanks and praise." Since mere humans are his earthly worshippers, imperfect gestures, words, musical phrases, and strokes of the artist's brush are all the means we have available; our challenge is to make of such gestures true worship, and compelling enough to induce a spirit of authentic worship in others. What is appropriate? Not less than our best. To achieve this true and acceptable praise, the finest craftsman's art has been apportioned to worship since God's instructions to Moses concerning the construction and adornment of the Tabernacle.[5] When we consider this archetypal passage we discover in great detail how nothing less than the best will do, and that beauty has a central role to play in the praise of God, beauty in both its physical and spiritual dimensions.

Can any praise be worthy of the Lord's majesty? No. Shall we then be silent? No. Because the redeemed heart is grateful, there will arise in grateful obedience a joyful outpouring of hearts, "a joyful noise unto the Lord," a singing, a poetry, a symphony of artistic expressions off all such beauty as He has made us capable, drawing us up a little closer to the unsurpassable beauty of his holiness.

Arts of the Holy

The manner of appropriate praise and worship is nevertheless a deeper and multifaceted question. Can there be worthy poetic praise of someone we love without imagery? (It is possible but exceedingly difficult and likely to be rather dull). We are familiar with the fact that poets commonly invoke the beauty of nature in praise of their human beloved. Robert Burns's "My love is like a red, red rose" serves as a homely example for many more elegant efforts; though

5. Exodus 25–31.

far less refined than Richard Wilbur's "The Beautiful Changes," (which also uses roses), the homeliness of the Scottish song may serve to remind us that in such praise, similes are inevitable.[6] Yet the God of the Hebrew Bible seems almost to rule out similes when Isaiah says, "To whom then will you liken God? Or what likeness compare to him?"[7] God speaks repeatedly through Isaiah, taunting the idol makers of Israel's neighbors, "To whom will you liken me and make me equal, and compare me, as though we were alike?"[8] These are clearly warnings in the spirit of the first commandment, against idolatry. God will not share his praise with another.

There is another manner of figurative speech in praise of God which seems, however, to be widely employed in Scripture itself, and to be as available to the visual artist as to the poet: metaphor. Some well-known biblical metaphors for God describe him as a rock, a fortress, or as a consuming fire—all metaphors which attempt to jar the mortal imagination toward conjuring with the strength and power of God, so infinitely superior to human strength. To take but the first of these, we see in the metaphor of the rock an enormous imaginative fruitfulness: "The Lord is my rock and my fortress and my deliverer";[9] ". . . and who is a Rock besides our God?";[10] "In you, O LORD, I seek refuge; do not let me ever be put to shame; in your righteousness deliver me . . . Be a rock of refuge for me, a strong fortress to save me."[11] All such figures are immediately meaningful in the context of desert warfare: "You are indeed my rock" has nonetheless a more general meaning of spiritual and emotional security.[12] This is the sense of the old hymn, "He hideth my soul in the cleft of the rock"; yet this rock is also that on which, Jesus says to Peter and his disciples, he will build his church.[13] It is also, as the apostles remind us, that rock on which some will stumble even while others find that same rock to be their refuge.[14] This is likewise the rock in which the wise man builds

6. Richard Wilbur, "The Beautiful Changes," 462.

7. Isaiah 40:18.

8. Isaiah 46:5.

9. Psalm 18:2.

10. Psalm 18:31.

11. Psalm 31:1–2.

12. Psalm 31:3.

13. Crosby, "He Hideth my Soul," 190. Matthew 16:18.

14. Romans 9:32–33, quoting Isaiah 8:14; 1 Peter 2:8.

his house,[15] and in all cases polysemously it is a living Rock, that rock in the desert struck by Moses from which flowed water, so that Paul can say "for they drank of the spiritual rock which followed them, and the rock was Christ."[16] The very multivalence of the image is a thing of beauty, and it is much the same for other biblical metaphors for God.

Relationally, God is Bridegroom, a lover, a Father, and so unsurprisingly, perhaps, a poet. When he speaks in the prophets, or in the book of Job, he does so in the finest poetry, even when he is angry.[17] Such metaphors led John Donne, the seventeenth-century poet and Anglican divine, to describe God as a "figurative . . . and a metaphorical God,"

> A God in whose words there is such a height of figures, such voyages, such peregrination to fetch remote and precious metaphors . . . such curtains of allegories, such third heavens of hyperboles, so harmonious elocutions . . . as all profane authors seem of the serpent that creeps, thou art the Dove that flies.

Donne goes on to say something yet more pertinent to our reflection here, namely that God is to be praised for the poetry of his creation (cf. Gk. *poeisis*, "making") and the beauty of the worship he has instituted:

> Neither art thou thus a figurative, a metaphorical God in thy word only, but in thy works too. The style of thy works, the phrase of thine actions is metaphorical. The institution of thy whole worship in the old law was a continual allegory; types and figures overspread all, and figures flowed into figures.[18]

It is the very character of a poetic God, himself a maker of all things beautiful[19] that prompts Donne to worship him with beauty in his Holy Sonnets, and to preach so poetically in his sermons. It is not merely the *facts* of God's acts and commands that prompt such lavish adornments of rhetorical beauty in praise of his goodness, it is the beautiful *style* and *manner* of God's speaking and artful gifting to the world that calls for emulation.

Donne is surely right to call our attention to the divine institution of worship as a point at which we may see into the character of God. In the biblical account it is not Moses who designs the Tabernacle but God himself.

---

15. Matthew 7:24.

16. 1 Corinthians 10:4.

17. See Jeffrey, *Scripture and the English Poetic Imagination*, chap. 1.

18. *John Donne's Devotions*, 125.

19. Ecclesiastes 3:11.

It is he who gives meticulous direction and prescribes that real artists are to be given charge over executing his commission.[20] It is clear in these directions that the finest available artwork is to adorn the sanctuary—beautiful tapestries, golden mountings carved with pomegranates, carved cherubim to frame the Mercy Seat and surmount the Ark, cherubim between whose wings the very presence of God would rest, sanctifying everything in the Holy of Holies.[21] Even the vestments of Aaron and the priests are to be adorned lavishly; as a sign of their holy purpose they are to be made "for glory and for beauty" (*chabod v' tipharet*).[22] Beauty, in short, is a signifier for the Holy, reflective of divine glory (*chabod*). In this way, beauty and holiness in the Bible are inseparably linked from early on, so much so that "beauty" (*tipharet*) and "holy" (*qodesh*) become almost interchangeable.[23] Thus, the call to "worship the LORD in holy splendor"[24] reaches its climax of response in the Psalmist's prayer: "One thing I asked of the LORD, that will I seek after: to live in the house of the LORD all the days of my life, to behold the beauty of the LORD, and to inquire in his temple."[25]

In this connection it is of no small significance that Hebrew is a language extraordinarily rich in terms for beauty—fourteen distinct words in all, far more than are available in Greek or Latin or contemporary western languages. *Tipharah* is one of those used to signify both the beauty of the Lord and also human beauty; *yapheh* is also used for both. *Tipharah* is connected directly to holiness in Exodus 28. *Yapheh* is used to denote the sexual beauty of women in Esther,[26] in the Psalmist's epithalamium,[27] and in the Song of Solomon,[28] but it is also used in reference to the king, "You are the most handsome of men,"[29] a passage applied by Christians to the beauty of Christ Jesus in a Messianic reading, which led to the familiar Jesuit hymn "Fairest Lord Jesus."[30] Even as he returns in judgment, the Messiah is *yapheh*,

20. Exodus 25–31.

21. Exodus 25:1–40.

22. Exodus 28:2, KJV.

23. Isaiah 28:5.

24. Psalm 29:2; 96:9; 2 Chronicles 20:21.

25. Psalm 27:4.

26. Esther 1:11; 1:7.

27. Psalm 45:11.

28. Solomon 6:4; 7:1.

29. Psalm 45:2.

30. This familiar hymn was composed as "Schönster Herr Jesu" by an unknown Jesuit

a figure of terrible beauty.[31] In a profound sense, God is the original and archetypal Artist, in all his works and words the very definition of beauty; to be made in the image of God implies a natural impulse to creativity and a recognition that human art is a high language of appreciation of divine art. Yet when Qoholeth pens his weary wisdom he writes:

> He hath made everything beautiful (*yapheh*) in his time; also, he
> has set eternity (*'olam*) in their hearts, so that no one can find out
> the work that God makes from the beginning to end.[32]

Our art can never, in the sense we may hope, achieve the same order of closure or satisfaction.

Yet what is the canonical anthology of Scriptures from Genesis to Revelation, creation to Last Judgment, except a witness to the holy glory of that One who said, "I am the Alpha and the Omega?"[33] After all, says the Psalmist, the cosmos itself worships, praising God "in the highest" from the very moment of creation itself: "The heavens are telling the glory of God" and, as that rich biblical poem goes on to say, there is no culture in which the proclamation of creational glory fails to be heard, even to the ends of the earth.[34] Yet with rare exceptions (e.g., Moses on Mount Sinai, Jacob wrestling with the 'angel,' Ezekiel's *merkabah* vision of the *shekinah chabod*) God is also a God who hides himself, so that it is possible for John to say, contextualizing the revolutionary character of the Incarnation, "no one has ever seen God"; the divine presence was heretofore clearly something more sensed than seen.[35] Now, in the divine eternal logos becoming flesh, something could be seen as well as sensed. Out of the deep blue-black of the cosmos (in Hebrew, also *'olam*) shone a brighter star, and its glory burst through the canopy of all that has been hidden behind the faintly speaking stars, one glorious Word, the very *Logos* or ordering principle of the universe, gloriously appearing in human form. This is the fundamental Christian concept beautifully expressed in Donald Jackson's marvelous incipit page for the Gospel of John. The burnished gold of the

---

and published in the *Munster Gesangbuch* in 1677. It was translated into English in 1873 by Joseph Seiss.

31. Psalm 33:7; Ezekiel 28:12; 17; 31:8; Zechariah 9:1; See Jeffrey, *In the Beauty of Holiness*, 25.

32. Ecclesiastes 3:11.

33. Revelation 1:8, 11.

34. Psalm 19:1.

35. John 1:18.

letters of John's prologue shine even more lavishly in the human form of God-man, the Word made flesh, declaring the glory of the Father in an unprecedented way.[36] The "figure" for the invisible God's intimate presence (*shekinah chabod*) suddenly became visible as a human form, something recognizable but charged with a transcendent difference: "and the word became flesh and lived among us, and we have seen his glory, the glory as of a father's only son, full of grace and truth."[37]

Historically speaking, the effect of the Incarnation upon human art has been transformative. Suddenly the old prohibitions against representing God melted away; because God became man in Christ Jesus, representing the Son was not only acceptable but desirable. The history of western visual art in particular has become a voluminous witness to this insight and to its corollary as suggested by Jesus to Philip: "Whoever has seen me has seen the Father."[38] Jesus, in himself, *shows* us the Father; the hiddenness of God is succeeded by the revelation of God's glory, and that in turn opens up a while new arena for praise and worship in the arts. Praise may henceforth aspire to worthiness in new ways.

Illuminated Bibles

The Jewish impulse to protect the hiddenness of God, to put "a fence around the Torah" by avoiding images, by obliquity in exegesis, by mastering forms of disclosure which at the same time both reveal and conceal, however faithful to orthodox readings of Torah, soon stood in sharp contrast to the Christian predilection for a proclamation that would be intelligible to all, literate or illiterate.

That became the justification for the use of images in debate with some eastern Christians as well as Jews, often now called iconoclasts, who held to the Jewish scruples. For Gregory the Great, perhaps the most influential Benedictine in the history of the western Church, artistic representations of biblical events functioned as a book for the illiterate[39]; following him, Benedict Biscop in England asks for images to be painted

36. John 1:1–18.

37. John 1:14.

38. John 14:8–11.

39. Gregory the Great wrote to the iconoclast Bishop of Marseilles about the year AD 600 to urge him to recognize the catechetical value of images to the illiterate poor. See Ayerst and Fisher, *Records of Christianity*, 2:101–2; Brown, "In the Beginning was the

so that everyone who entered the church, even if they could not read, whenever they turned their eyes, might have before them the amiable countenance of Christ and his saints, though it were but in a picture, and with watchful minds might revolve on the benefits of the Lord's incarnation and having before their eyes the perils of the last judgment, might examine their hearts the more strictly on that account.[40]

The third canon of the Fourth Council of Constantinople (869–870 AD) reiterated the point:

Just as all men receive salvation from the syllables contained in the gospels, so do all men, learned and ignorant alike, receive their share of that boon through the channel of the colored images placed under their eyes.[41]

In this statement we see the beginnings of an important move from a purely catechetical or didactic justification to suggest that there is a gift to all through the attractiveness of "colored images placed under their eyes." This reference may be directed in particular to the images that had increasingly been adorning special copies of the Bible, or parts of it, from the sixth century on. Benedictines were heavily involved.

The beauty of some of these manuscript Bibles, adorned with the finest artistry of medieval painters, is breathtaking for most who see them for the first time. They also reflect diverse artistic styles and cultural iconography. The Garima Gospels manuscript, executed in the upper Nile with splendid Ethiopic east-African images and iconography of the sixth century, is dramatically different from the lavish purple-backed, gold leaf inscribed text and Latinate images of the Vienna Genesis, but both indicate something beyond merely a desire to instruct.[42] These are Bibles created for beauty; the finest artwork was dedicated to their adornment because someone, artists or patrons, thought that the Scriptures were of such value that they commanded the richest, most beautiful adornment possible. Such artwork was a sign of praise and veneration for the texts, which were employed ceremonially in worship as a means of offering up beauty in the service of holiness.

Word," 4.

40. *The Historical Works of the Venerable Bede*, 353.

41. Gilson, *Arts of the Beautiful*, 164.

42. See the excellent illustrated study by McKenzie and Watson, *The Garima Gospels*; see also *The Vienna Genesis*, with an introduction and notes by Emmy Wellesz, with selected reproductions.

Similarly, the Lindisfarne Gospels, executed about 725 AD by Benedictine scribes and artists in the north of England, had clearly more intended purpose than their presentation of the Latin text and interlinear Anglo-Saxon translation. They were a treasure for the altar, as was the Book of Kells.[43] To read from such Bibles in the liturgy would have been a high honor.

Later Bible illustrators followed suit, and produced monuments of beautifully illuminated Scripture such as the *Bible Moralisée* of the thirteenth century,[44] but, in a surprising development, illuminated Torahs and Haggadah manuscripts for use in Jewish synagogues also appeared throughout Europe.[45] In all these cases the beauty of the artwork far exceeds the requirements of function. Not only does the beauty of the page prompt slow and meditative reading and reflection; it is also a source of recurrent wonder and pleasure. The Word of God is seen as a treasure, a beautiful gift of God's grace that compels thanks and praise; this is a book fit to be honored above all other books. The devotion of King Alfred the Great to his copy of the text was such that he commissioned a magnificent jeweled pointer resembling a Jewish *yad* (one of several such to have survived), called in Anglo-Saxon an *aestel*. Records made clear that its creation at great cost was a tribute in honor of the biblical text.[46]

Perhaps the last great example of biblical illumination was a facsimile, the Gütenberg Bible of 1455. Printed on paper, it has illustrated capitals, and it was nevertheless in many of its copies hand colored so as to give the appearance of an illuminated manuscript Bible.[47] (Actually, given the costs of its production it was almost as expensive.) Since then, the emphasis in printed Bibles has been utility and, as the costs of printing fell by the seventeenth century, the Bible was wisely made more available for private ownership, with a consequence that the idea of creating a Bible to be a thing of beauty in its physical appearance gradually faded away.[48] *The Saint John's Bible* is a notable recrudescence of the older tradition, in which Benedictine artists have long played a major role.

---

43. Brown, *The Lindisfarne Gospels*.

44. Laborde, *La Bible moralisée illustrée*, 5 vols.

45. Jeffrey, "Manuscript Illumination in Medieval Hebrew Bibles," 66–72.

46. Hinton, *The Alfred Jewel*.

47. See Davies, *The Gutenberg Bible*.

48. An exception would be the illustrated Bibles so popular in the nineteenth century. See the chapter by Sue Sorensen, chapter 5 in this book.

Beauty as Gift

If the Hebrew Bible is so rich in beauty words, it can come as a puzzlement that the New Testament lacks anything like a comparable range. Only four instances of a single Greek word are to be found in all of the New Testament which may be unambiguously translated as "beauty," and all four are instances of a single Greek word, *horaios*, a term which in classical Greek had denoted "ripeness," or "fittingness." Two of these occurrences are adjectival and refer to "the gate called Beautiful" (of the Temple) by which Peter and John effected a healing for the man blind from birth. A third instance, also adjectival, is St. Paul's translation of the now liturgical phrase from Isaiah 52:7, "How beautiful are the feet of those who bring good news"[49] in which *horaios* translates Hebrew *na'ah*, one of the least common of Hebrew words for beauty. The fourth and final instance of the Greek word occurs in a distinctly unpleasant context, when Jesus rebukes religious disingenuousness, saying, "Woe to you, scribes and Pharisees, hypocrites! For you are like whitewashed tombs, which on the outside look beautiful, but inside they are full of the bones of the dead and of all kinds of filth."[50] *Horaios*, in any of these uses, suggests the beauty of appearances. What, we may ask, has happened to suppress so rich a vocabulary for beauty in the Old Testament?

There are two *prima facie* reasons. The first of these, as I have explained elsewhere, is that the Greek of the first century, like the Greek of the Septuagint Bible, had very few available terms for beauty—perhaps four at most.[51] The second is that beauty terms in Hebrew were still in use by the early Christian community in the language of Jewish Christian worship and the Hebrew Scriptures themselves, all still normative for Jesus and the apostles, none of whom used Greek on a daily basis—except Paul, later, in his ministry to the Gentiles. But there is a third factor, partly philological and certainly theological, which turns out to have had a great and enduring compensatory significance for Christian tradition: a highlighting of spiritual beauty. The most common Greek word for beauty, *kalos/kalon*, is appropriated by Plato at the end of his *Phaedrus*, when he has Socrates pray for "inward beauty"; this is the only prayer in all of Plato's extant works,

49. Romans 10:15.
50. Matthew 23:27.
51. Jeffrey, *In the Beauty of Holiness*, chapter 1.

and it suggests an aspect of beauty that will in fact become important in Christian tradition, though not via Plato.[52]

Strikingly, the normative Greek word for beauty, *kalos*, is to be found all over the New Testament, but almost exclusively to signify "good" in the sense of moral good, not aesthetic appeal. To take but two examples: when Jesus refers to himself as "the good shepherd [who] lays down his life for the sheep,"[53] the phrase is *o poimên o kalos*; speaking in Hebrew or Aramaic, Jesus would have likely said, *tov*, the same word which occurs in Genesis where God after each day's artistry, "saw that it was good." In Paul's first letter to Timothy he urges that new Gentile converts not be obligated to Jewish food laws, since "for everything created by God is good"[54] (*panktisma Theou kalon*), another creational echo. Of the many other instances of *kalos/kalon* in the sense of "good," the context of holy worship is prevalent.[55] Among these is the narrative in Matthew's gospel in which a woman who is reputedly not "good" pours out a bottle of expensive perfume on the head of Jesus.[56] Not all present approve of her act as a "good work," but Jesus defends her against the accusation of Judas that her perfume should have been sold and the proceeds given to the poor, saying "she has wrought a good work' (*ergon . . . kalon*) upon me.[57] The RSV and EV translations have done better in translating Jesus' response to her spontaneous act of worship as "she has done a beautiful thing to me." It is this sense of the beauty of good deeds, enacted beauty, that will gradually emerge as a New Testament distinctive. In fact, Jesus here points us already in this direction, adding, "By pouring this ointment on my body she has prepared me for burial."[58] The unnamed woman does "a beautiful thing" for the One who will presently do the most beautiful thing ever, giving up his very life out of love for the Father and love for those he came to redeem. This is surely the paragon example of "beauty which will save the world."

Beauty as a deed, the beauty of gift, has several exemplars in the Bible, but we should not go far wrong if we saw three as pivotal for our subject, and a fourth and fifth as descriptive of beauty in response to the harmony

52. See the discussion by Jaeger, *Paideia*, 2:194.

53. John 10:11, 14.

54. 1 Timothy 4:4.

55. Jeffrey, *In the Beauty of Holiness*, 33.

56. cf. Luke 7.

57. Matthew 26:10, KJV.

58. Matthew 26:12.

of divine gift. The three divine gifts of beauty are Creation, Incarnation, and Redemption; on this point I think most Christian theologies agree. Each receives, accordingly, a beautiful feature illumination in *The Saint John's Bible*. Of the other two instances of beauty in reference to action, the first is the explicit call for beauty to be apportioned to worship in the book of Exodus already mentioned. The art and liturgy there described sets a pattern for Jewish and Christian thinking about what it is to respond to "the giver of every good and perfect gift"[59] with holy worship, praise, and honor which in some measure is the best our creativity can offer. In the apt words of seventeenth-century poet and priest George Herbert, such art is itself a response to answered prayer:

> Thou hast granted my request,
>> Thou hast heard me;
> Thou didst note my working breast,
>> Thou hast spar'd me.
>
> Wherefor with my utmost art
>> I will sing thee,
> And the cream of all my heart
>> I will bring thee.[60]

Herbert speaks for all seriously Christian artists in these lines. The other story, a favorite of Christian poets and painters, is the one in Matthew 26 or its parallel in Luke 7 of the broken-hearted and repentant courtesan whose tears and costly ointment are alike poured out in rejection of her former life and grateful worship of her Savior. The Lord regarded this as a 'beautiful thing," a gift of sacrifice and embodied, adoring worship. This commendation, I would suggest, identifies the character of inner beauty, beauty enacted, taking our eyes off mortal beauty altogether and attuning us to a higher register of the Beauty from which it derives.

---

59. James 1:17, KJV.

60. Hutchinson, ed., *The Works of George Herbert*, 146; see also his "Praise III," effectively a taking up of Augustine's opening question in his *Confessions*, with which we began here (157–59). In the newer edition by Wilcox, *The English Poems of George Herbert*, "Praise II" appears with pertinent notes on 506–8.

The Saint John's Bible Crucifixion Page

How can the torture and execution of an innocent man be perceived as a subject of beauty in art? On the face of it, this seems not merely incongruous but preposterous. It was certainly no metaphor; the bloody reality of it has often galvanized painters into shockingly lifelike representations (e.g., Matthais Grünewald's center panel for the Isenheim Altar). In that light the resplendent glory of Christ on the Cross in *The Saint John's Bible* Luke Gospel, radiant with gold and shedding a golden glory even over the place of execution and the chaos of a troubled world, might seem to some to have missed the point (see Figure 9, *Crucifixion*). I think not, however.

One understands the uneasiness of early Roman Christians with the image of a crucifixion, even as symbol. This was the form of execution for slaves, reserved for the most shameful death by torture the Romans had devised. Its equivalent today would not be a gallows or electric chair, but a medieval rack or iron maiden. The cross does not appear in any of the myriad Christian catacomb frescoes, nor does it appear in early church art before the late fourth century.[61] The habilitation of the Cross as a Christian symbol associated with worship and the décor of beautiful churches came slowly into view during the fifth century, and when it did, suddenly the cross was visually transformed, bedecked with jewels or surrounded by a radiance of mosaic splendor. Evidently the ugly cross had been transfigured into something now indicative of a beauty that was not physical, but spiritual.

The leading theological influence on this new artistic realization appears to have been St. Augustine. In his sermons he argued that just as God's own "immutable Beauty" is reflected in his Creation in such a way as all recognize,[62] so too in the Incarnation God's invisible beauty became manifest in human form, a theological conception well expressed in Donald Jackson's incipit page for the Gospel of John. For Augustine, the incarnate God is "beautiful in heaven, beautiful on earth, beautiful in the womb, beautiful in his parents' arms," and even "beautiful upon the Cross."[63] This is as much as to say that the immutable Beauty of God which he gave expression to in his Creation and redemptively in his Re-creation, begun with the Incarnation, is somehow gathered to a point of radiant fullness in the

---

61. See Jeffrey, *In the Beauty of Holiness*, chap. 2, for a full discussion.

62. Augustine, Sermon 241.1.1, p. 116.

63. Augustine, *Ennarationes in Psalmos* 44.3; cf. 45.7, pp. 146, 148.

Atonement, his self-offering in Jesus on the Cross being the culminating point of God's self-disclosure in a beautiful deed. Thus, for Augustine, it is entirely fitting to speak of the Cross as beautiful. The willingness of God-in-Christ to be "deformed," made ugly by his torture and death on the cross, is, he says to his congregation,

> What gives a form of beauty (*formosa*) to you. If he had been unwilling to be made ugly, you would never have gotten back the beauty you lost. So he hung on the cross, deformed, but his deformity was our beauty (*sed deformitas illius pulchritrudo nostra erat*).[64]

Such a costly gift of beauty demands a response from us in kind, for "he loved us first who is always beautiful, and by loving him we are in turn made beautiful."[65] For Augustine, that response begins when with the eyes of faith, a Christian comes to see the unparalleled beauty of God's self-offering for sinful men and women.[66]

Since Christ never abandoned, even in his disfigurement on the cross, "that beauty which is in the form of God,"[67] transcendent Beauty itself, the very glory of God, shines through the "form of one who hung upon the cross," transfiguring it with eternal radiance. This seems to me to be precisely what Jackson has captured in his majestic plate for the Crucifixion.

How may an artist show a beauty which is transcendent, given that the transcendent is itself invisible? How should an artist depict a beauty which is there for the eyes of faith, but invisible to those outside of the experience of grace? How can the idea expressed so persuasively by St. Augustine be translated into a perceptible vision of "that beauty which is in the form of God"? Though *The Saint John's Bible* is everywhere a gift of beauty, especially for any who cherish God's central redemptive action in Christ Jesus on the cross, and who remember it in community when they worship, its pinnacle achievement theologically seems to me to be its representation of the Crucifixion. Jackson shows the Cross as an effusion of divine glory, bursting upon the world in a radiance which transfigures not only the cruel instrument of execution (on the viewer's left) but also the faces of those who look to the Cross as a sign of hope (lower right). They are a diverse folk gathered from the ages, some awestruck, others

64. Augustine, Sermon 27.6, cited in Harrison, *Beauty and Revelation*, 234.

65. Augustine, *Tractates on the Gospel of John*, translated by John W. W. Rettig, 9.9, 257.

66. Comment on Psalm 128:8 in Augustine, *Tractates on the Gospel of John* 2.1.

67. sup. Psalm 104:5.

shaping toward prayer, and one figure who recalls the John the Baptist of many crucifixion paintings, pointing to Christ, the Lamb of God who takes away the sins of the world.[68] The lavish gold leaf of the Cross itself, and the radiant beams which pour out unconstrained across the sky, turn the ugliness of Christ's death on the literal cross to transformative spiritual beauty. In the Cross alone is all our glory, says this work; in the Cross alone the fullness of God's eternal glory becomes irrefragably known to all who have eyes to see. Dividing the crescent-mooned cosmos, the starry sky on the left, the firmament which so long has declared the glory of God,[69] from a world below which is now a New Creation in Christ, is the singular act in all human history which inverts all prejudices and expectations, converting our sorrow into everlasting joy. This work is a masterpiece of the Bible illuminator's painterly art, an apt demonstration that beauty in the Bible transforms our every imagination of beauty, making us long for the beauty of holiness from which it arises and to which it points. In contemplating this image, we are drawn into something very like an epiphany; this beautiful cross signifies a new Holy of Holies, a *santum sanctorum* from which the glory of the Lord does not depart.

Bibliography

Augustine, Saint. "Sermon 241.1.1." Translated by Erich Przywara. In *An Augustine Synthesis*. London: Sheed & Ward, 1939.

———. *Confessions*. Translated by R.S. Pine-Coffin. New York: Barnes & Noble, 1992.

———. *Ennarationes in Psalmos*. Translated by Cleveland Cox. In *Nicene and Post-Nicene Fathers*, ser. 1, vol. 8. 1888. Reprint, Peabody, MA: Hendrickson, 1994.

———. *Tractates on the Gospel of John*. Translated by John W. Rettig. 5 vols. Washington DC: Catholic University of America Press, 1988.

Ayerst, David, and A. S. T. Fisher. *Records of Christianity*. Vol. 2. Oxford: Blackwell, 1977.

Bede. *The Historical Works of the Venerable Bede*. Translated by Joseph Stevenson. London: Seeleys, 1853.

Brown, Michelle P. *The Lindisfarne Gospels: Society, Spirituality and the Scribe* Toronto: University of Toronto Press, 2003.

———. "In the Beginning Was the Word: Books and Faith in the Age of Bede." *The Jarrow Lecture*. Newcastle-upon-Tyne, 2000.

Crosby, Frances J. "He Hideth My Soul." In *Evening Light Songs*. Nashville: Faith Publishing House, 1949.

Davies, Martin. *The Gutenberg Bible*. London: British Library Board, 1996.

68. John 1:29.

69. Psalm 1:1–2.

Donne, John. *John Donne's Devotions upon Emergent Occasions, together with Death's Duel.* Ann Arbor: University of Michigan Press, 1965.

Gilson, Étienne. *Arts of the Beautiful.* New York: Scriber, 1965.

Harrison, Carol. *Beauty and Revelation in the Thought of St. Augustine.* Oxford: Clarendon, 1992.

Herbert, George. *The English Poems of George Herbert.* Edited by Helen Wilcox. Cambridge: Cambridge University Press, 2010.

———. *The Works of George Herbert.* Edited by F. E. Hutchinson. Oxford: Clarendon, 1944. Reprint, 1972.

Hinton, David A. *The Alfred Jewel and Other Late Anglo-Saxon Decorated Metalwork.* Ashmolean Handbooks. Oxford: Ashmolean Museum, 2008.

Jaeger, Werner. *Paideia: The Ideals of Greek Culture: Volume II: In Search of the Divine Centre.* Oxford: Oxford University Press, 1986.

Jeffrey, David Lyle. *In the Beauty of Holiness: Art and the Bible in Western Culture.* Grand Rapids: Eerdmans, 2017.

———. "Manuscript Illumination in Medieval Hebrew Bibles." In *The Book of Books: Biblical Canon, Dissemination and Its People.* Edited by Jerry Pattengale, Lawrence M. Schiffman and Filip Vukosavovic. Jerusalem: Bible Lands Museum, 2013.

Laborde, Alexandre. *La Bible moralisée illustrée, conservée à Oxford, Paris, et Londres.* 5 vols. Paris: Pour les membres de la Société, 1911–1927.

McKenzie, Judith S., and Francis Watson. *The Garima Gospels: Early Illuminated Gospel Books from Ethiopia.* Oxford: Manar al-Athar, 2016.

Wellesz, Emmy. *The Vienna Genesis.* London: Faber & Faber, 1960.

Wilbur, Richard. "The Beautiful Changes." In *Collected Poems 1943–2004.* Orlando: Harcourt-Harvest, 2004.

3

Should Bibles Be Beautiful?

How Beauty Teaches Us to Pray

MATTHEW A. ROTHAUS MOSER

MANY OF US CAN identify with the young St. Augustine who, long before "saint" was attached to his name, expressed his distaste for the Bible. Compared to the beauty and sophistication of his favored Latinate philosophy and literature, the language and the stories of the Bible struck him as aesthetically displeasing and morally abhorrent.[1] Like the young saint, we often approach the Bible and find ourselves at turns dazzled, moved, frustrated, and befuddled. Inasmuch as the Bible plays a central and governing role in the Christian faith, it remains a deeply mysterious book, not easily understood. Those who dare to open its pages enter a strange world. We are immediately confronted with the difficulty of having to learn the Bible's language, even if we are reading it in translation. We find that it is not only the *language* of the Bible but also the entire world of the text—its ideas, metaphors, assumptions, and foundational claims—that requires translation. Learning to read the Bible is like learning a new language: we must move slowly, patiently, and humbly through the text, gradually acquiring greater fluency in the Bible's strange ways. This is the work of a lifetime, as

---

1. "I therefore decided to give attention to the holy scriptures and to find out what they were like. And this is what met me: something neither open to the proud nor laid bare to mere children; a text lowly to the beginner but, on further readings, of mountainous difficulty and enveloped in mysteries. I was not in any state to be able to enter into that, or to bow my head to climb its steps . . . It seemed to me unworthy in comparison with the dignity of Cicero," *Confessions* 3.5.9.

the old cliché goes, for when it comes to the language of the Bible, we are always beginners and never experts.

And yet, just as we discover when we study a new language that our world is expanded and enriched, when we learn the strange language of the Bible's world, we find opening up before us an eternal horizon. As Jeremy Begbie notes, when we "get inside" a new language, we end up discerning and understanding more about the world that has heretofore been familiar to us.[2] Similarly, as we learn the strange language of the Bible, we find our understanding of ourselves, of our world, and of God gradually expanding, increasing, taking on new and unexpected depths.

What should we call this slow labor of learning the language of the Bible, this relentless broadening of our understanding of its divine depths and its meaning for us today? In this essay, I suggest that the ancient practice of *lectio divina* (holy reading) provides a useful model for this patient labor of learning how to read and understand the Bible. Moreover, in concert with Rowan Williams' claim that *The Saint John's Bible* "gives insight into that lost skill of patient and *prayerful reading*,"[3] I demonstrate ways that the art of *The Saint John's Bible* can provide a new avenue of prayerful reading which can foster the spiritual practice and art of *lectio divina*.[4] In this way, I will suggest that the art of *The Saint John's Bible* serves as a "vehicle of discovery"[5] or a mode of exploring the depths of the Bible, the fruit of which is the expanded and enriched understanding of God's own beauty, goodness, and truth as revealed in Scripture. But this understanding is not purely conceptual or intellectual. The understanding that *lectio divina* issues in is transformative. To put it another way, the art of *The Saint John's Bible* is not merely ornamental, but has the potential to initiate readers through the transforming practices of *lectio divina* to the contemplation of God in the "beauty of holiness."[6] We might thus understand the theological work of *The Saint John's Bible* as bringing beauty, prayer, and love together in the contemplative unity of the life of God—the life into which practices of *lectio divina* are meant to lead.

2. See Begbie's introduction to *Beholding the Glory*, xi.

3. See the introduction to the present volume; emphasis mine.

4. For those interested in practicing *lectio divina* with *The Saint John's Bible*, there are a set of resources available to assist with what they term *visio divina*; see "Seeing the Word."

5. Begbie, *Beholding the Glory*, xi.

6. Psalm 96:6

Art, Incarnation, and the Danger of Idolatry

For some, my claim that beauty can teach us to pray may be controversial. How can we justify praying the Bible through the art of *The Saint John's Bible*? Is it not tantamount to idolatry to suggest that contemplation of human art can lead to contemplation of God? How can finite form(s) disclose the eternal and infinite God? If God is spirit[7] and cannot be represented in any graven image,[8] shouldn't we aim for purely "spiritual" worship that transcends finite form?

Despite gnosticizing tendencies to the contrary,[9] Christian knowledge of God has always emerged from the encounter with the eternally transcendent God who makes himself known *in* and *through* finite form. It was the formless God who appeared to Moses in the particular form of the burning bush, who guided Israel through the desert as a pillar of smoke and fire, who displayed Godself to Ezekiel through the images of thrones, beasts and wheels, and who finally dwells fully and bodily among us in Jesus Christ.

Christians must understand beauty through the logic of the incarnate Christ. Hans Urs von Balthasar says that God's beauty is "splendor" that shines through finite forms without being reducible to them. Beauty can be a revelation and a theophany: a sudden shining, an outburst of splendor, glory, and goodness that makes the transcendent present to us within finite form.[10] Christ's incarnation grants to the historical and particular an infinite and eternal meaning. In Christ "dwells all the fullness of God bodily."[11] Christ is the "concrete universal;"[12] his flesh is the site where history and materiality are caught up into the eternal life of God. In Christ, all of history takes on meaning and becomes significant, that is, all history signifies or points to the God present within it.

In Christ we witness the presence of the universal *in* the particular. This provides the theological grounding for our contemplation of physical beauty. Rather than the sensual materiality of the arts being an idolatrous distraction from contemplation of the eternal God, it is precisely in and

7. John 4:24.

8. Exodus 20:4.

9. Eugene Peterson, *Christ Plays in Ten Thousand Places*, 59–62.

10. Von Balthasar, *Seeing the Form*, 20–28.

11. Colossians 2:9

12. William Cavanaugh, *Being Consumed*, 77ff.

through the tangible, the particular, and the material that we find disclosed to us the eternal, invisible, and transcendent. In light of the incarnation, art can function less as idolatry and more as theophany.

Lectio Divina and the Manifold Meaning of Scripture

The term *lectio divina* means "divine reading" and has roots in the early Christian Fathers, especially such notable figures as Origen, Ambrose, and Augustine. In these early fathers of the church, practices of reading Scripture were loosely correlated with an understanding of the Bible as having multiple layers of meaning, or what is often called the different "senses" of Scripture. While the details vary from author to author, these four senses are typically presented today as the literal, the allegorical, the tropological or moral, and the anagogical or unitive senses. As the church fathers knew well, practices of *lectio divina* can help readers of Scripture enter into the multidimensional meaning of the biblical text, and it is precisely here, I am suggesting, that the illuminations of *The Saint John's Bible* come in to lead us into prayer, transformation, and holiness.[13]

The practices of *lectio divina* emerged in more systematic form in the early and high middle ages, especially in the Benedictine tradition—the same tradition that gives us *The Saint John's Bible*. These practices were part of the threefold structure of Benedictine life: liturgical prayer, labor, and prayerful reading of Scripture. Physical labor and prayer were both understood to bear the fruit of holiness in the life of the monk.[14] This is the Benedictine rhythm of *ora et labora*, prayer and work. The unity of prayer and physical labor bears spiritual fruit.

Though the artisanal labor of *The Saint John's Bible* is not quite the same as cultivating fields, they participate in the same spiritual logic. Prayer is not simply the abstract work of the mind and intellect. Rather, prayer incorporates the entire person by drawing mind, body, and imagination into the contemplation of God. The structure of Benedictine life ties reading, prayer, and physical labor together in much the same way that, as we shall see, *The Saint John's Bible* holds these aspects together in a single reality of divine contemplation.

13. For a modern iteration of the tradition of *lectio divina* and the spiritual senses of Scripture, especially as they relate to theological aesthetics, see von Balthasar, *Seeing the Form*, 365–407.

14. Benedict, *The Rule of St. Benedict*, chapter 48.

But what exactly is *lectio divina*? In general, *lectio divina* unfolds according to a fourfold order. The first stage is reading, *lectio*; the second is meditation, *meditatio*; the third prayer, *oratio*; the final is contemplation, *contemplatio*. Each stage in *lectio divina* draws the reader deeper and deeper into the text, gradually conforming her entire person to Scripture through her ever-expanding practice of prayer.

Consequently, this prayerful reading is a way that modern Christians can translate the strange language of the Bible into our contemporary lives. Moreover, as I seek to show in what follows, the beauties of *The Saint John's Bible* can play an important role in nurturing this prayerful, contemplative performance of the Bible.[15] To that end, I take each of the four stages of *lectio divina*, explain them and their association with the senses of Scripture, and explore how the art of *The Saint John's Bible* (in particular the frontispiece to the book of Genesis) might offer us a contemporary pathway into the practices of *lectio divina* and the contemplation of God.

Lectio

Lectio simply means reading. It means attending to the text as it comes to us. *Lectio* is attention to the literal sense of the text, focusing on the presentation of the historical narrative at hand in word and image. We can perform *lectio* on the St. John's Bible by focusing our attention to the forms, shapes, colors, beauties, and harmonies of its art. Attending to the physical construction of the images before us attunes us to the presence of beauty in those particular forms that make up the image at hand.[16]

Within the framework provided by the incarnation of Christ, attention to the crafted images of *The Saint John's Bible*—to the shapes, colors, and techniques of their representations—is not a form of idolatrous attention to graven images, but rather a "close scrutiny of the way in which [images] are functioning in the text."[17] Such close scrutiny develops in

15. A caution: Christian theological aesthetics must always guard against a simplistic or naive celebration of beauty lest we fall into an overly-romanticized theology of glory that would soften or sanitize the scandal of Christ's cross. Christian beauty cannot be reduced to "comeliness" or "good taste." Beauty in the Christian sense is the glory of crucified love; aesthetic pleasure alone is inadequate for a Christian conception of the beautiful.

16. On the need for aesthetic and spiritual attunement, see Balthasar, *Seeing the Form*, 246–48.

17. Evans, *The Language and Logic of the Bible*, 70.

us disciplines of slowness and attention—the same intellectual and spiritual dispositions that are necessary for *lectio*.[18] By inviting us to slowness and attention, *The Saint John's Bible* offers us a profound gift. While the studied familiarity with biblical stories might tempt us to read quickly and inattentively, the representations of *The Saint John's Bible* force us to slow down by making the familiar strange. It takes stories and ideas that are so familiar to us that they have become tame and easily digestible and re-presents them to us in new and unexpected ways, allowing us to see and understand the text anew.

For example, Genesis 1's narrative of creation is entirely commonplace for most contemporary readers of the Bible. The tale of Elohim creating the world over the course of seven divine days has become so entrenched in our cultural imagination, its meaning so blandly domesticated, so predictable, that the story itself becomes opaque to us. Our familiarity with the story actually limits our ability to see it for what it is: a shocking claim that the world that we inhabit, filled as it is with tragedy and heartbreak, is made *good* and ordered to God's beauty, peace, and rest. In the face of our callousness, the art of Genesis 1 in *The Saint John's Bible* takes the story, renders it strange and therefore visible to us again (see Figure 1, *Creation*). This is part of what it means to call *The Saint John's Bible* an "illuminated" manuscript. The art sheds new light on the familiar story, letting us see it again as if for the first time. Its strangeness slows us down, forcing us to pay attention to what our familiarity bids us skip over.

Let us consider the Genesis frontispiece in more detail as a *practicum* in *lectio*. When we attend closely, several things immediately catch our eye: the most obvious, perhaps, is the image's partition into seven equal segments that represent the seven days of creation. We notice at once that the seven partitions have significant artistic differences. These differences in color, tone, shape, and even movement, nevertheless work together to present a balanced, complex, and harmonious whole. We also note the presence of the Hebrew word *tohu-wabohu* ("formless void") in the bottom left corner: the chaotic, surging "deep" over which the spirit of God hovers, and from which God forms the harmony of creation.

Our *lectio* of the image also draws our attention to the unexpected arrangement of the golden squares throughout the text. We notice that the

---

18. On our need for formation in attention, and the role education plays in that formation, see Weil, "On the Right Use of School Studies in View of the Love of God" in *Awaiting God*, 21–30.

golden squares are associated with the seventh partition, the Sabbath day of divine rest and the presence of God. Their arrangement across the image conveys a sense of double movement. If we read the image from left to right, we notice the arrangement of seven golden squares across the seven days of creation. As we follow their movement across the image, our eyes follow their trajectory upward as they ascend gradually to unity, a single golden square, in the seventh day. If we are to read the image from right to left according to the conventions of the Hebrew language, we follow the movement of the golden squares from unity descending into multiplicity.

The last features of the Genesis frontispiece to which I want to attend in this practice of *lectio* is the suggestive movement of the raven across days three, four, and five, coupled with the coiled presence of the snake on day six. While a more theological reading of their presence in Genesis must await the work of *meditatio*, it is worth noticing how their presence destabilizes a simplistic and naive understanding of Genesis 1.

The presence of the raven in flight calls to mind the spirit, or *ruāch*, of God, hovering over the waters of creation. Yet the fact that it is a *raven* (rather than, say, a dove—in anticipation of the baptism of Jesus scene), is suggestive. The raven is often associated with prophecy—indeed, it was the raven that was said to bring God's messages to St. Benedict. So, despite the representation of God simply as the golden light of the seventh day, the raven is nevertheless suggestive that this is a God who *speaks*, who does not remain locked up within the holy silence of eternity, but communicates Godself in and to the world.

The presence of the snake may also be a surprise. For one, the infamously crafty serpent of Genesis 3 is here represented as being part of the unreservedly "good" creation of Genesis 1. This perhaps unsettles the assumption that Genesis 3's serpent is somehow a representation of Satan, a primordial force of evil that wrecks the divine goodness of creation. Here even the serpent receives God's pronouncement that "it is good." We must, then, find a way to understand the story of the Fall and its legacy of sin and death, anticipated here in the presence of the snake, as somehow caught up within the larger framework of the sheer, unmitigated goodness of God's creative act.

Meditatio

Meditation on the text is the second stage of *lectio divina*. It marks a clear boundary between what was considered the literal or historical meaning of Scripture and its spiritual senses: the allegorical, moral (or tropological), and unitive (or anagogical). We can draw a loose association between the practices of *meditatio* and the allegorical sense of Scripture before we return to our contemplation of the Genesis frontispiece.

Meditatio is a discipline of presence and patient waiting. We must sit with the text, attending to it with our full attention, dwelling with it.[19] It involves imaginatively entering into a text, learning to inhabit it, conforming ourselves to its words, narrative, and logic. In meditation we must resist our desire to dictate the meaning of Scripture, narrowing its meaning into neatly organized, easily digestible concepts. To meditate means "to chew" on a text the way a cow chews on its cud: slowly and with great deliberation. Meditation considers the text from beginning to end—taking it in, chewing it, swallowing it—and then doing this all over again.[20] Each time you go through the process of meditation, the text takes on new and richer meaning.

Moving from *lectio* to *meditatio* means creating space in oneself that allows the Holy Spirit to move freely, slowly and patiently expanding and enriching our sense of the text. Meditation requires a degree of humble receptivity, waiting for the Holy Spirit to illuminate the meaning of the text under consideration. In meditation we offer ourselves as students awaiting instruction from a voice other than our own. We approach the Bible in a spirit of charity and surrender. In meditation, our attention becomes so invested in its object that we become utterly consumed by it: "*si pense tant que il s'oblie*"—he thinks until he himself is forgotten.[21]

Moreover, meditation means placing yourself within the text, inhabiting it, binding yourself to it. This is where readers begin to understand the

---

19. On the idea of attentively dwelling with the object of contemplation and its implication for literary criticism and higher education, see Michael Martin, *The Incarnation of the Poetic Word*, 7ff.

20. See the painting by Marc Chagall entitled "Meditation" in which Chagall presents a rabbi meditating on scripture alongside a cow chewing the cud. My gratitude to David Lyle Jeffrey who brought this painting to my attention in a conversation several years ago. For his reading of this painting, see Jeffrey, *In the Beauty of Holiness*, 330–35.

21. Chrétien de Troyes, *Le Roman de Perceval, ou Le Conte du Grand*, cited in Martin, *The Incarnation of the Poetic Word*, 8.

text within a larger framework, yet one that draws them personally into the text in transformative ways. What is this larger framework? We might say that *meditatio* turns our attention to the larger framework of the Bible's allegorical sense. Here, we understand things in relation to other things. As we enter into the Bible through *meditatio*, we find depths of meaning and signification open up before us. *Meditatio* opens up new modes of perception. As Johann Goethe wrote, "Every object, well contemplated, opens a new organ of perception in us."[22] We begin understanding allegorically as we are illuminated by the Spirit who "searches out the deep things of God."[23]

Allegory involves the transferal of meaning from one thing to another. The movement of allegory is "sideways, from one thing in the created world to another."[24] The allegorical sense of Scripture is still tightly connected to the literal sense; allegory addresses those things "which have really taken place, but which prefigure the form of some other mysterious thing."[25] What the allegorical sense of Scripture prefigures and discloses to us is the mystery of Christ. For example, the church read the episode of the Israelites at Marah where Moses casts a branch of a tree into the bitter waters making them sweet[26] as a prefiguration of the way Christ's cross heals the bitterness of our sin.

With this in mind, we return to the Genesis frontispiece and practice *meditatio*. As already mentioned, the significant differences between the seven days nevertheless work together in marvelous harmony. This harmonious balance of the image illuminates the poetic balancing of Genesis 1: the balanced coupling of heaven/earth, night/day, sky/land, etc. and draws us into the inner sense of Genesis 1's repeated refrain that "it is good." Moreover, given that the "goodness" (*tōv*) of creation in Genesis 1 is an aesthetic term, the balanced representations of *The Saint John's Bible* offer us a special glimpse into the theology at work in the account of creation. Imaginative meditation on this harmony lifts our understanding up to consider the nature of God as creator, the peaceful arranger of cosmic elements, the director of all things to their end in the light of the Sabbath day.

What of the ascending and descending movement of the golden squares across the image? We recognize that the gold represents the

22. *Scientific Studies: The Collected Works*, vol. 12, 39.

23. 1 Corinthians 2:10

24. Evans, 121.

25. Ibid.

26. Exodus 15:23–25

presence of God and the in-breaking of eternity into history. When we imaginatively enter into their movement across the page, we find ourselves caught up in the grand movement of creation as *exitus-reditus*, the movement of God's love downward in the act of creation and upward in the act of redemption. The simple presence of these ascending and descending golden squares captures the entire movement of the Christian story—and of creation itself—as the movement from God and to God in the dynamic movement of divine love.

Furthermore, our imaginative meditation on the golden squares can support the allegorical connection between Genesis and the Gospels. The descending and ascending movement of the golden squares in the Genesis frontispiece suggest the descent of God the Son in the incarnation of Christ, depicted in the frontispiece to the Gospel of John as a golden figure descending from heaven into the cosmic order. The Genesis image thus anticipates John's description of the *Logos* as the one "through whom all things were made."[27] Meditation on the golden squares in the Genesis frontispiece prepares us for the encounter with Christ who descends to us in birth and death so that we might share his resurrection and ascension. Creation and redemption are thus iconically linked. Our meditation on Genesis leads naturally to a meditation on the God who creates *and* redeems the world. We enter imaginatively into what St. Athanasius described as "fittingness": that the one through whom the world came into being should also be the one through whom the world was restored to God.[28] Indeed, such understanding provides the theological framework for the work of *lectio divina*; we find ourselves here meditating on the very source and cause of our meditation.

What of the raven and the snake? As a figure associated with prophecy, the raven suggests the God who speaks and is not silent. The raven is, perhaps, illustrative of God's creating word that says to the void "let there be . . . ." and there is. As an icon of God's word, the raven anticipates yet again John 1's *Logos* through whom all things are made. The raven shows that the divine Word is not abstract and ethereal, but is at one and the same time the self-expression of God and the very life of the world. The Word

---

27. John 1:3. One might also think of the image entitled *Crucifixion* found in the gospel of Luke. It also depicts Jesus all in gold, again reinforcing both his divine identity and his presence in creation.

28. See Athanasius, *On the Incarnation*, 1.1.

that takes on flesh and dwells among us as Christ Jesus is also the Word that undergirds and gives life and meaning to all things.

The raven is also presented in such a way that captures its rapid movement across—or more specifically *up*—the image, again representing creation's movement toward God as its source and goal. More importantly, the raven captures the union or harmony of the creation, for the bird inhabits land and sky and thus represents the union of creation in its movement toward the peace and rest of the Sabbath day. The peaceful rhythm of birds in flight anticipates the eternal rest of the Sabbath, giving us the image of the natural ordering of things according to what John Milbank calls an "ontology of peace."[29] Creation is not fundamentally or essentially violent and chaotic but rather akin to the peacefully directed movement of a bird in flight.

Likewise, the image of the serpent is dense with allegorical meaning. Given its role elsewhere in *The Saint John's Bible* (especially in the image entitled *Adam and Eve*), the serpent is certainly meant as a harbinger of the Fall in Genesis 3. We might interpret the serpent's presence here in the seven days along the lines of a dualism that sees evil as an inherent part of creation, intrinsic to our reality—the serpent is a worm that gnaws away at creation's core. But this is perhaps not the best way to interpret the serpent's presence here. Recall that in *meditatio* we read according to the allegorical sense and thus we look at our text (in this case, the image of the serpent) through the mystery of Christ.

During his late-night conversation with Nicodemus in John 3, Jesus recalls the story of Moses fashioning and raising up a bronze serpent to deliver the Israelites from the bite of poisonous serpents.[30] "And just as Moses lifted up the serpent in the wilderness," Jesus tells Nicodemus, "so must the Son of Man be lifted up, that whoever believes in him may have eternal life."[31] Scripture itself testifies to the densely layered meaning of serpent imagery, and it is precisely this multi-layered meaning that animates the image of the serpent in the Genesis frontispiece. Considered allegorically—that is, christically—the serpent in the Genesis image anticipates and iconically represents both our Fall and our redemption. Indeed, the

29. See John Milbank, *Theology and Social Theory*, 278ff.

30. This story can be found in Numbers 21:8–9. I'm grateful to Daniel Train for bringing these connections to my attention.

31. John 3:14–15

frontispiece depicts a human figure trampling the serpent,[32] a prophesy of Christ's crucifixion and his harrowing of hell.

It is only in the mystery of Christ's redemption that the mysteries of creation, humanity, and sin take on light.[33] Christ himself is revealed to us through our meditation on the Genesis frontispiece; it is through Christ that we begin to understand the allegorical meaning of Genesis.

Oratio

Though the entire agenda of *lectio divina* is oriented toward prayer, it is in *oratio* that praying the text becomes the explicit focus and task. While different traditions within Christianity may emphasize different kinds of prayer at this stage, it is commonly held that in *oratio* we offer up the fruits of our *lectio* and *meditatio* as our personal words of praise and confession to God. In *oratio*, the text becomes a mirror, a way of seeing ourselves and offering ourselves to God by making use of the words—or in the case of *The Saint John's Bible*, the images—of Scripture. To adopt the words of St. Gregory the Great, "Scripture is set before the eyes of the mind like a kind of mirror so that we may see our inward face in it. For therein we learn about our deformities and our beauties."[34] In *oratio*, Scripture becomes our speech and we listen carefully as through it God speaks.

We might connect practices of *oratio* with the moral or tropological sense of Scripture. This is where our reading directly intersects with our lives, where we hear God's word addressed directly to us in our immediate situation. It does this, Evans suggests, "by putting the examples of others before us; we are stirred to follow their example, and helped to resist the vices ourselves by the realisation that they have fought the battles we are now fighting against the vices and have conquered them."[35] As our *oratio* intersects with the tropological sense of Scripture, we find the strange world of the Bible gradually translated into the context of our real life.

How might we practice *oratio* with *The Saint John's Bible*? If we treat the Genesis frontispiece as a mirror of the self, we are immediately drawn into the juxtaposition between the ordered harmony of the seven days

32. Genesis 3:15

33. Second Vatican Council, *Gaudium et Spes*, par. 22.

34. Gregory the Great, *Moral Reflections on the Book of Job*, 2.1.1. See also Evans, 120.

35. Evans, 120.

and the disorder and cacophony of our lives. We see ourselves as the disordered *tohu wabohu*, and seek the presence of God hovering over our chaos, (re-) creating us from the mess of our disorders. As we prayerfully attend the image, we are confronted with the various particularities of our lives through which we undermine the original goodness of God's creation. Each of the seven days in the Genesis frontispiece conveys creation's original goodness; our prayerful reading of those images elicits our own confession of our own deformities and our shared responsibility in deforming the world's original goodness.

Prayerful consideration of the raven, perhaps a representation of the *ruach*, or breath of God, hovers over creation, connecting heaven and earth. We recall to mind the vocation of creation to be the house of God, where God's spirit rests. Yet, confronted by the disorder which shrinks the capacity of our lives to bear God's presence, we pray with St. Augustine, "The house of my soul is too small for you to enter: make it more spacious by your coming. It lies in ruins; rebuild it."[36] Nevertheless, the presence of the snake shows that the house of creation—the house of the soul—is rife with potential rebellion, a desire to question God's authority over us, to set ourselves up as our own gods.[37] The image holds up a mirror in which we see and know the truth of ourselves as broken yet still made good and ordered to God. But since the serpent also anticipates our redemption, we offer up our hopeful confession to Christ who is ready to save us.

Thus the tropological sense of the image evokes such confessional prayers from us; these prayers are the fitting response to the tropological meaning of the movement of the image's golden squares: they represent our own movement away from God in sin and our return to God, drawn by the lure of God's grace. Such confessions serve as our way of entering into the restlessness of creation's longing for God as its final resting place.

Contemplatio

Finally, we come to *contemplatio* or contemplation. This is where reading, meditation, and prayer carry us into transformative encounter with the living God. This is the purpose of studying the Bible: the love of God in Christ, or what St. Augustine calls wisdom (*sapientia*). Wisdom is identical with love, or charity (*caritas*). Contemplation is thus the loving enjoyment

36. *Confessions* 1.5.6

37. See Dietrich Bonhoeffer, *Creation and Fall*, 104–106.

of God that comes about by means of our intellectual and spiritual pursuit of truth; it is where we are drawn into the life of God. This is where we become what we were truly meant to be: image-bearers of God, reflecting and embodying the wisdom and love that God is.

This turn to contemplation reminds us that understanding the Bible does not consist primarily in the acquisition of information *about* it. Understanding the Bible involves the *formation* of the soul and the *conformation* of the mind and the soul to Jesus Christ—the way, truth, and life,[38] whom we meet through the pages of Scripture.

Contemplatio corresponds to the anagogical sense of Scripture, which the Catechism defines as viewing "realities and events [in the Bible] in terms of their eternal significance, leading us toward our true homeland: thus the Church on earth is a sign of the heavenly Jerusalem."[39] It is when God's eternity breaks through the finitude of text and image, attuning us to the divine life. If the tropological sense understood Scripture as a mirror in which we see our beauties and deformities, the anagogical sense, coupled with our practice of contemplation, transforms us into the mirror, enabling us to reflect God's truth, beauty, and goodness outward into the world with grace and love. It is here that our reading and our prayer flower into charity, as we come to share in the divine love that is the life of God.

It is at this point, however, that analysis, description, and theory fall silent. How the images of *The Saint John's Bible* might speak in the contemplative mode and carry us into the presence of God eludes the power of language to capture or describe. All that can be said is that in *contemplatio*, we find ourselves caught up in the movement of those golden squares—the in-breaking of God's presence into our lives—drawing us, through Christ, into the golden light of God's presence, where the first word and the last word of our created lives is "it is good" precisely because our entire selves are united in love and grace to God. This union with God is not an assimilation of ourselves into God that results in a kind of monism. It is, rather, the perfect harmony of difference, where creation and Creator come together in the embrace of love, beauty, and goodness. *Contemplatio* occurs when we know ourselves as created—that is, as embraced in the perfection of divine love and transformed into the divine image. It is in contemplation that we find ourselves illuminated by

38. John 14:6
39. *Catechism of the Catholic Church*, par. 117

the splendorous beauty of God and participating in the grace-filled word of God that shines out in creation and redemption.

While we might not be able to speak about the inner reality of contemplation, we can perhaps consider the fruits of that contemplation: the divine gift of charity. That charity is the summit of contemplation should not be particularly surprising to us; if we are united to the God who *is* love, it follows that we come to share more and more fully in God's own love.[40] According to St. Augustine, the fruit of the study of Scripture is charity: the love of God and the love of neighbor.[41] Any interpretation of Scripture that teaches true charity is therefore a correct interpretation of Scripture. This is the goal of *lectio divina*: to enjoy God and love one's neighbor on account of God. What is important, though, for Augustine, is that Scripture's teaching is not something intellectual or conceptual. No, properly reading—and teaching—Scripture actually *cultivates* charity: one does not simply *know* about charity, one *becomes* charitable. If contemplation is where we are illuminated by the light of God's love, the fruit of that contemplation is when *we* become the illumination that makes God's love present and visible to the world.

"Understanding" the Bible Today

What does it mean to "understand" Scripture today? According to Rowan Williams, to "understand" something is to know what to do or say next—much like the way we express our understanding of a sequential pattern by discerning the word that correctly follows.[42] The proper "understanding" of Scripture is measured, not by our ability to parse its language, analyze its narrative, or systematize its theology. Understanding the Bible consists rather in knowing what to say and do next. That is, the proper understanding the Bible consists in prayer and charity. Such understanding is not easily bought; it demands the ceaselessly active surrender of our entire selves. It pulls our

40. There is a lovely meditation on this in Dante's *Paradiso* 21. Dante is among the contemplatives and he encounters Peter Damien in a beam of divine light. Within the luminosity of Damien's shining, Dante sees that his perfect contemplation has transformed him into the divine love that has been the object of Damien's contemplation. On this, see Vittorio Montemaggi, "Contemplation, Charity, and Creation *ex nihilo* in Dante's *Commedia*."

41. Augustine, *On Christian Teaching*, 3.36.

42. Rowan Williams, *The Edge of Words*, 79.

entire selves—our attention, imagination, our conscience, our brokenness, and our love—into transformative encounter with God.

Who can see God and live? the Scriptures ask. No one can see the face of God and live—or at least not live the same way as one always has. The fruit of contemplation is the radical transformation of the entire self, our entire life, so that it is no longer we who live but Christ who lives in us.[43] This is the work of *lectio divina*. Ultimately, the movement of our holy, prayerful reading of Scripture involves the translation of this strange, ancient text from the distant and closed-off past into the vicissitudes, challenges, and demands of divine charity in our present moment. But even more than that, the translation of our reading becomes the translation of our very selves, caught up in the descending and ascending movement of God's love for creation. All too often, this meaning is lost to us today, whether through a calloused familiarity with the Bible or an incomprehensibility of the Bible's strange and opaque language. And yet, if this is the inner heart of the meaning of the Bible, then the art of *The Saint John's Bible* retrieves the Bible's strangeness and significance for our modern age, offering us new ways into the destabilizing and transformative beauty, goodness, and truth of God's love.

Bibliography

Athanasius, Saint. *On the Incarnation*. Edited by John Behr. Yonkers, NY: St. Vladimir's Seminary Press, 2012.

Augustine, Saint. *Confessions*. Translated by Henry Chadwick. Oxford: Oxford University Press, 1998.

———. *On Christian Teaching*. Translated by R. P. H. Green. Oxford: Oxford University Press, 2008.

Balthasar, Hans Urs von. *Seeing the Form*. The Glory of the Lord: A Theological Aesthetics 1. Translated by Erasmo Leiva-Merikakis. Edited by Joseph Fessio and John Riches. San Francisco: Ignatius, 1982.

Begbie, Jeremy, ed. *Beholding the Glory: Incarnation through the Arts*. Grand Rapids: Baker Academic, 2001.

Benedict, Saint. *The Rule of Saint Benedict*. Edited by Timothy Fry. New York: Vintage, 1998.

Bonhoeffer, Dietrich, *Creation and Fall: A Theological Exposition of Genesis 1–3*. Translated by Douglas Stephen Bax. Edited by John W. de Gruchy. Dietrich Bonhoeffer Works 3. Minneapolis: Fortress, 1997.

Catechism of the Catholic Church. http://www.vatican.va/archive/ENG0015/_INDEX. HTM.

43. Galatians 2:20.

Cavanaugh, William T. *Being Consumed: Economics and Christian Desire*. Grand Rapids: Eerdmans, 2008.

Dante, Alighieri. *The Divine Comedy*. Edited by David H. Higgins. Translated by C. H. Sisson. Oxford: Oxford University Press, 2008.

Evans, G. R. *The Language and Logic of the Bible: The Road to Reformation*. London: Cambridge University Press, 1984.

Gregory the Great, Saint. *Moral Reflections on the Book of Job*. Vol. 1. Translated by Brian Kerns. Cistercian Studies Series 249. Collegeville, MN: Liturgical, 2014.

Goethe, Johann. *Scientific Studies*. Collected Works 12. Princeton: Princeton University Press, 1995.

Jeffrey, David Lyle. *In the Beauty of Holiness: Art and the Bible in Western Culture*. Grand Rapids: Eerdmans, 2017.

Martin, Michael. *The Incarnation of the Poetic Word: Theological Essays on Poetry and Philosophy; Philosophical Essays on Poetry and Theology*. Kettering, OH: Angelico, 2017.

Milbank, John. *Theology and Social Theory: Beyond Secular Reason*. 2nd ed. Oxford Blackwell, 2006.

Montemaggi, Vittorio. "Contemplation, Charity, and Creation *ex nihilo* in Dante's *Commedia*" in "Creation *Ex Nihilo* and Modern Theology," ed. Janet Martin Soskice, special issue, *Modern Theology* 29.2 (2013) 62–82.

Peterson, Eugene. *Christ Plays in Ten Thousand Places*. Grand Rapids: Eerdmans, 2008.

Second Vatican Council. "Gaudium et Spes," 1965. http://www.vatican.va/archive/hist_councils/ii_vatican_council/documents/vat-ii_const_19651207_gaudium-et-spes_en.html.

"Seeing The Word: Visio Divina with *The Saint John's Bible*." http://www.seeingtheword.org/.

Weil, Simone. *Awaiting God: A New Translation of* Attente de Dieu *and* Llettre à un Religieux. Translated by Brad Jersak. Abbotsford, BC: Fresh Wind, 2013.

Williams, Rowan. *The Edge of Words: God and the Habits of Language*. London: Bloomsbury, 2014.

4

Beauty Cannot Be Rushed

An Invitation to Contemplation
from *The Saint John's Bible*

ROBERT MOORE-JUMONVILLE

IF SOMEONE ASKED YOU to hold your hand up in the configuration of a backward C, it might signify several things. It could be a gang sign, or a signal to an alien spacecraft, or a symbol of the ancient figure Pac-Man. If you could square the edges of your hand, it would look like the second letter of the Hebrew alphabet, the *bet*, as in *alef-bet*. *Bet* also denotes the Hebrew preposition "in" and it is the first letter of the Hebrew Bible, the Torah—"*in* the beginning," or "*when* God created." Moreover, since Hebrew reads from right to left, the mouth of the *bet* points in the direction which the first sentence of Scripture flows.

All that may seem unimportant, but not so for Rabbi Akiva-ben Joseph, one of the leading contributors to the Mishnah, a religious sage who died in AD 137. Rabbi Akiva would strongly affirm the religious significance of this Hebrew letter: "You think any part of Scripture can be without meaning?" he might exclaim. "Of course not! Here, I'll tell you what it means: Our friend, the *bet*, instructs us: 'Israel's God is shrouded in mystery and we must seek him.' But where do you think we can possibly find the Almighty? If we have eyes to see, our friend the *bet* declares the answer. He tells us plainly: 'Do not look behind you in history. Do not seek God above the earth, or God forbid under the earth!'" Akiva would playfully show with his finger how the *bet* points forward into the Torah: "Here is the path of life, the Way, in

43

these words of Scripture." He might go on to say to us today: "So make time to see God here, in the Holy Scriptures, but only so you can better recognize God in the world around you: God's face in the face of your neighbor; God's shape in the fold of the landscape around you; God's goodness in a simple meal or cup of coffee."[1]

Akiva was no biblical literalist, not a scholar who strove to narrow Scripture as an end in itself—into a rival god to be worshipped. No, he understood Scripture as a means to an end. Just as medicine is a means to health, so Scripture is a means to salvation, and a pathway for communion with God. Those who have crafted *The Saint John's Bible* would agree with Rabbi Akiva that their illuminated text of scripture serves as a means to an end, a means of grace, urging us to seek God. Two assumptions quickly become evident: first, God often appears as hidden, and second, we must learn to seek Him—through scripture, through prayer, through praying the scriptures.

When we look at *The Saint John Bible's* illuminations of the *Word Made Flesh* from John 1, or of the *Transfiguration* of Jesus with Moses and Elijah on either side of him, we encounter Christ as simultaneously luminous and concealed in mystery—as though the very brightness of his being blurs our vision (see Figure 6, *Transfiguration*). In the portrayal of John the Baptist, in the *Baptism of Jesus* illumination, the Baptist walks toward the viewer while looking over his shoulder at a distant crowd along the Jordan. Christ stands in the center, a silhouette of burnished gold against the backdrop of the ordinary crowd. In the *Road to Emmaus* illumination, we find two depictions of the risen Christ. While the first shows Christ in the lower right foreground shrouded in muted shapes of mostly red, the second, in the upper left corner, depicts him shining in gold swirling lines as he breaks bread with two disciples he has met on the road, just prior to his vanishing from their sight. In other words, the first image shows Christ cloaked in humanness, the second shows him cloaked in divinity.

But straightaway the question surfaces: Why is God hidden? In the first place, it may not be that God hides, but rather that human beings cannot perceive God when he is present. As one hymn frames it poetically: "Holy, holy, holy: though the darkness hide thee, though the eye of sinful man thy glory may not see." That is our human condition: we are spiritually blind, like those souls in Plato's cave parable. We are chained, facing a wall,

---

1. This reflection on Rabbi Akiva came out of a class on early exegesis I had with Karlfried Froelich at Princeton Theological Seminary in 1983.

only able to perceive shadows, unaware of the deeper reality around us that is infused with Spirit.

Theophilus of Antioch compared our condition to the seeds in a pomegranate rind—because we are enclosed in the rind of ourselves, we cannot see objects outside of us. Just so, we are enclosed in all creation within the hand of God: "It is he whom you breathe, and you do not know it! For your eye is blind, your heart hardened. But if you wish, you can be cured. Entrust yourself to the doctor, and he will open the eyes of your soul and your heart."[2] We might consider *The Saint John's Bible* as a medicine, then—an instrument, a salve, used by our mystical doctor to cure spiritual vision.

Yet, beyond our human limitations, it seems God also chooses to remain hidden, freely shrouded—on the other side of a Cloud of Unknowing. But why? Perhaps because human beings are inveterate idolaters? God remains disguised within the world—because he knows we tend to turn him into something small and petty and self-serving (into something I manipulate for my benefit—enlisting God to promote my cause). As Church Father, Gregory of Nyssa argued: "Every concept formed by the intellect in an attempt to comprehend and circumscribe the divine nature can only succeed in fashioning an idol, not in making God known."[3]

How quickly we turn God into something manageable—into an abstraction—or worse! In C. S. Lewis's *The Screwtape Letters*, Uncle Screwtape instructs his nephew, the junior tempter Wormwood, to encourage human beings to affirm ownership—and then to extend that ownership to God:

> We teach them not to notice the different senses of the possessive pronoun—the finely graded differences that run from 'my boots' through 'my dog', 'my servant', 'my wife', 'my father', 'my master' and 'my country', to 'my God'. They can be taught to reduce all these senses to that of 'my boots', the 'my' of ownership. Even in the nursery a child can be taught to mean by 'my Teddy-bear' not the old imagined recipient of affection . . . but . . . 'the bear I can pull to pieces if I like'. And at the other end of the scale, we have taught men to say 'My God' in a sense not really very different from 'My boots', meaning 'The God on whom I have a claim . . . , whom I exploit from the pulpit.'

2. Clement, *Roots of Christian Mysticism*, 27.

3. Ibid.

45

This is why Lewis wrote: "The prayer preceding all prayers is 'May it be the real I who speaks. May it be the real Thou that I speak to'"–because so often, even in our sincerest prayers, we turn God into something less than God.[4]

And yet another question emerges, related to God's hiddenness: a pesky one, that we might rather avoid. Let's assume God is hidden and that, to connect with God, we must seek him. Why, then, do we not seek him? Why are we so half-hearted? Pascal's *Pensée 149* might help elucidate what I mean. First, let me paraphrase the end of Pascal's statement: God could overcome the doubts of the most hardened skeptic by showing up, revealing himself in the way he will appear at the Last Day "with such thunder and lightning and such convulsions of nature that the dead will rise up and the blindest will see him." However, that would be like a teacher handing out "A" grades to students who never did their reading and always slept through class. So, on the one hand, it was not fitting for God to appear in such a way that those who do not deserve his mercy would be convinced beyond a doubt (almost against their will). But on the other hand, it was not fitting for God to hide himself so thoroughly that those who earnestly sought him could not find him if they tried. "Thus wishing to appear openly to those who seek him with all their heart, he has qualified our knowledge of him by giving signs which can be seen by those who seek him and not by those who do not."[5] It seems we should learn to know the signs, then.

But let me ask again why we do not seek God? At this point, it seems best to admit honestly that not everyone is interested in the question of God's presence or absence. Often we are much too distracted to care. In the fall of 2016, Jim Triggs, Executive Director of the Heritage Program, came to Spring Arbor University to speak to faculty and students about the wonders of the Saint John's Bible. For these campus lectures, professors often bribe students to attend through offers of extra credit, so admittedly the commitment level varies. I took a photo on my phone of Mr. Triggs in front of an enormous screen showing the fabulous panels of the creation illumination. Later I noticed in my photo that the student two rows in front of me was on her laptop scrolling through Pinterest. What a comment on our civilization. We might conclude that atheism is not as dire a threat to Christian culture as is indifference. Here sat a student paying for a college education, blinded to the stunning beauty in front of her by what—inspirationally captioned cat photos and T-shirt logos? The photo of this student

4. Lewis, *The Screwtape Letters*, 114; Lewis, *Letters to Malcom*, 82.

5. Kreeft, *Christianity for Modern Pagans*, 68–69.

illustrates our incessant distraction, our fear of empty spaces and silence. By the way, how many times have you checked your cell phone since you started reading this chapter? Social media and cell phones clearly symbolize the restless state of our souls.

Perhaps this stands as one of the most common features of our generation: we are frantic but too terrified to slow down. Let me quote someone who has put our post-modern stress in lyrical form:

> There's no hiding for me
>
> I'm forced to deal with what I feel
>
> There is no distraction to mask what is real
>
> I could pull the steering wheel
>
> I have these thoughts so often I ought
>
> To replace that slot with what I once bought
>
> 'Cause somebody stole
>
> my car radio
>
> And now I just sit in silence.[6]

Oh, how our media fixations promise to save us from any painful self-examination.

Of course, our modern fear of silence lurks deep in the heart of the human condition. On the one hand, human beings are finite, fallible, fragile, and dependent. Life makes us tremble, so we welcome distraction. On the other hand, God appears as wild, inscrutable, and sovereign. Put those two truths together and you have a recipe for anxiety. We call out. Yet often God remains hidden. And we shudder at the prospect of being alone, orphaned by the universe. It is true, God does give us a name by which to address him—the Sacred Name, but this Holy Name of God cryptically reads: "I am who I am." It's a name retaining divine freedom and purity. God says, "Here is my name; don't take it in vain. Don't yank my chain."

We all complain that we find ourselves too busy; that we have too much going on. But, in fact, we have way too much time on our hands—so much so, that we try to numb ourselves through entertainment and distraction and hurry. We want distraction, precisely so we do not have to face our dire human condition—as creatures vulnerable, afraid, alone, driven, empty, and anxious. Peter Kreeft suggests:

---

6. Twenty One Pilots, "Car Radio."

We want to complexify our lives. We don't have to, we want to. We want to be harried and hassled and busy. Unconsciously, we want the very thing we complain about. For if we had [more time], we would look at ourselves and listen to our hearts and see the great gaping hole in our hearts and be terrified, because that hole is so big that nothing but God can fill it.[7]

We are touching, here, on experience that relates to the biblical Fall of human beings as depicted in Genesis 3 and the subsequent Christian teaching on original sin. Ponder for a moment, in this context, how easily the Devil might manipulate human anxiety. Imagine, for instance, the story of sin in the Garden of Eden. God is not there at the time. He is out finishing up a galaxy. In the meantime, he has left Adam and Eve alone in the garden. He only arrives later to find Adam and Eve covering their shame with leaves: "Adam, where are you?" God asks. But picture, as the curtain rises on the opening scene, Eve sitting by herself, perhaps feeling isolated, even desolate. "Where is everyone? Where is God? Where is Adam?"

Up slinks the serpent (with malice aforethought). Give him a sinister Peter Lorre accent: "Where is this God of yours? Maybe he's abandoned you? Why has he left you alone? You shouldn't trust him! He's not letting you in on things. He's holding back. But . . . if you eat this fruit, you'll be . . . a god yourself. You'll be strong like him. You won't need to worry any more about being afraid—no more fear of pain, or privation, or loneliness, or insecurity, or loss of control. Here, hurry, reach for this . . . enchanted elixir." Now consider what it would have been like if Eve merely had insisted that she and the serpent sit and wait for God to return. Before Adam ever shows up, imagine that the Serpent has Eve cornered, alone. Only this time, Eve takes a slower, more contemplative, approach—not letting the serpent (who is dressed in sheep's clothing) rush her into buying anything.

> Serpent: You should eat this fruit
>
> Eve: God told us not to
>
> S: Did he say, Don't eat any of it?
>
> E: No, just from *this* tree
>
> S: Why do you think not this one?
>
> E: I've no idea; you think maybe he's planning on sending it out? You know, to get the tree cleaned?

7. Kreeft, *Christianity for Modern Pagans*, 168.

S: I think he wants it all for himself.

E: You know; you look awfully stressed.

S: Doesn't that fruit look good?

E: Yes, but there are lots of trees we can eat from. I know, let's take a tour. I'll show you some really great fruit trees. Some are really sweet, others tangy. . .

S: But this fruit will make you wise: really, really, really smart.

E: Maybe you think too much.

S: I do have a lot of grand ideas—like the Nazis.

E: Are you getting enough sleep? Your eyes are all bloodshot. . . . I know, let's wait for Adam to come back and we'll ask him to help us decide.

S: No, we definitely cannot WAIT!

E: We could sing some hymns while we're waiting

S: Ugh I hate hymns. . . . One day, I'm going to invent worship choruses. . . . Don't you think you should eat this fruit before it's too late? You'll miss out on your one great chance to be like God.

E: Funny thing, we already are like God, made in his Image and all.

S: Hurry, eat it; Now! Someone is coming!

E: Calm down, Mr. Slide. . . . Why do you have to be in such a hurry? I know. . . . We could wait for God and ask him what he wants us to do with this tree's fruit. How about that? Have you ever played Euchre?

At the core of all temptation swirls a spirit of impatience, a spirit that grows agitated with silence—or when faced with too much emptiness, or solitude. This evil, lying spirit whispers, "This is not enough. It will never do. You are abandoned and rejected. So, quick, hurry now—before it's too late. Don't wait. It'll be gone: taste it, make it happen. Buy it now! Grab the kiss. *Carpe diem*."

In contrast, the tradition *The Saint John's Bible* flows out of encourages us to slow down and take a deep breath. If you have had the privilege of handling *The Saint John's Bible* Heritage edition, you know that you simply cannot rush through its pages—it does not come in digital. It does not come equipped with a clicker or a remote. Twice I have had the privilege of taking home the "Gospels and Acts" volume for the weekend to use at our church and I can tell you that the size and weight of this single volume alone are considerable. When the book looks up at you from the couch, it does not shout: "I'm portable. Let's do a multi-task." Nor does it whisper, "Hurry up! Read me now. Quick!" Instead, it murmurs: "Pssssst. Calm down. Take it easy. Sit with me. Let's stay awhile." The weight and texture of the pages, as you turn them, say "slow down," like a good back rub should be given, or like flecks of snow flakes falling and swirling in a breath of breeze. *The Saint John's Bible* experience is tactile. Sensory.

The illuminations themselves become like texts—something one has to read thoughtfully. Colors within a single illumination combine in a way that say, "Let's linger here for some deep breathing." One cannot flippantly run through the pages. In a video interview, Alan Reed (who was a member of the Committee on Illuminations and Texts) said of *The Saint John's Bible*, "It's so against everything the culture is about right now: easy, consumerism, use-and-toss." He is referring to our throw away culture, right? Then he adds: "We've had some complaints from people that this is hard to read. And we say, 'No it's not hard to read, it just slows you down.' Which is what you want people to do when they're meditating on these images and these words."[8] For it is only when we slow down, that we are able to touch the finitude of our humanity with compassion; only then can we begin to admit our vulnerability, and at the same time declare: *This* is enough. Beauty cannot be rushed. In fact, we can go even further and insist that nothing that is fully human can be rushed: neither birth, nor growth, nor learning, nor virtue, nor love, nor death. And our human search for God certainly cannot be rushed either.

Perhaps reading and meditating on an illuminated manuscript like *The Saint John's Bible* includes an ethical dimension—for this kind of reading slows us down, and slowing down is a necessary ingredient for choosing well, and wisely. If that is true, no wonder advertisers endorse the quick image over the slower, more complex painted contemplative version of the word. No doubt, we could come up with exceptions of inspiration that flash instantly on the mind, like Handel's *Messiah*. But it is not humanly prudent to go forever rushing out one's door looking for something more, something better, some greener grass past the far fence.

8. *Saint John's Bible,* Brother Alan Reed.

I'm reminded of a cartoon I once saw that shows Christian Martians who have landed. They have gotten out of their spaceship, goggling around with big eyes. I imagine they are on a mission from their Church Board, because the caption reads IN SEARCH OF GREENER "PASTORS." A dissatisfied culture scurries around looking everywhere for answers in the wrong places, leaving home to find something better. Maybe the reason people are leaving their homes, their churches, and their marriages in record numbers today has something to do with our fear of really being known. When we slow down in life, with people who have lived with us for years, they know our shortcomings, and remind us of our finitude and failures. Being known makes us nervous. So we bolt.

Beauty, in contrast, takes time. The creation of *The Saint John's Bible* took over fifteen years. Consider how long it takes for a human being to become beautiful and what they look like in the end of that process. For beauty implies staying put, being rooted, placed on common ground. From one of the universities I served emerges a story that has taken on mythic proportions: The Power Outage of '05. An ice storm blew into town in February, 2005, knocking out the power grid on a cold wintery day. Cell phone technology and satellite coverage still remained somewhat primitive. With no lights, classes were temporarily canceled, but since no one knew when power would go back on, people stayed on campus. If class cancelations had been announced ahead of time, for instance, people who lived close by would have gone home. Others would have left for neighboring towns looking for entertainment. But since no one knew when classes would resume, people stayed. Two dorms broke out into their annual snowball war and a window was broken. Huzzah!!! People lined up on the campus sledding hill.

For warmth, students crowded into the snack bar and huddled together in dorm lounge rooms. For several years afterwards, students would look wistfully as they remembered: "We had nothing to do, no technology, so we just hung out and talked like it mattered." In Chesterton's novel, *Manalive*, one of the characters exclaims with passion: "If we were snowed up in this room, we'd be the better for reading scores of books in that bookcase that we don't even know are there; we'd have talks with each other, good, terrible talks, that we shall go to the grave without guessing."[9] When we do begin to slow down, one of the things we discover is that human beings come in

9. Chesterton, *Manalive*, 291.

beautiful shapes and that life can fill with joy, *if* we take the time to notice. Because—as we all know—beauty cannot be rushed.

Of course, we always want more out of life. We want greener grass over the next fence; we want greener groceries; greener technology; we want greener bodies; we want to be saplings, forever. Because what we have right now certainly is not enough. In his novel *Hannah Coulter*, Wendell Berry offers a beautiful example of receiving life as "enough," an example which incidentally serves to underscore how dissatisfied most of us normally live. In a crucial line in the book, Hannah exclaims: "Members of Port William are not trying to 'get someplace.' They think they are someplace." In fact, looking for a better place, Hannah muses, means you'll likely end up in a worse one. Nor do you ask to be given a different life with a different man. You accept the one you've got and make it good. Early in the book, Hannah sets up this refrain as she reflects on the happiness of her young life with her Grandmam: "We had everything . . . but money." "It was a good enough life too."[10]

If we are afraid we do not have enough, we will likely start to get anxious; and anxiety tends to make us speed up. Is it because we somehow think slowness amounts to mental if not moral deficiency; like when the person in the car in front of us has the audacity to drive the exact speed limit! Obviously, there is something wrong with a person like that! The smart person, the urbane sophisticate, knows how to get everything done quickly. I love *The New Yorker* Cartoon showing two men in a jungle, waist deep in what is obviously quicksand and sinking. The sophisticated man looks at the other, who is dressed as a park ranger, and carps: "In New York, we wouldn't call this quick."[11]

About fifteen years ago, I began leading my junior level spiritual formation class through an exercise the first day of class. Sometimes I teach four sections a year, and it is a general education requirement, so I have led numerous students through this drill. I hand out an apple to each person in the class and say: "Take out a piece of paper. My directions will be intentionally minimalistic. Tell me everything you can about this apple." Fifteen years ago students could last twenty to twenty-five minutes before they grew restless and gave up. This last week, they lasted six minutes. The time frame, their attention span, gradually has shrunk that much. It might be worth interpreting the stages students go through during the exercise. Most

10. Berry, *Hannah Coulter*, 83, 109, 14.

11. Liam Walsh.

recently, they look at their apple, get close up with one eye closed like they are peering through a microscope, and jot down five to eight bullet points: "round, green, bent stem, not really round, brown spots." After about four minutes, these days, they start to throw glances at their neighbors, checking to see if they are still invested. When they feel they have written enough (always painfully sparse), they begin looking out the window, then at the clock, then at me. At first they smile. "What more do you expect," they seem to ask with their eyes. Finally, a few glare at me with eyes that accuse: "You're evil. Stop this torture." Students currently experience six minutes of concentrated attention as overly onerous.

Americans always seem to want some sort of quick magic formula, something that gets "it" done faster—as though life were a race. When I was growing up, the so-called experts told nursing mothers they had discovered something superior to their own milk—FORMULA! Many American mothers started replacing their own milk with formula! Sure, it was faster, but we know how that worked out—we got the Baby Boomers, the most dissatisfied of all American generations! Fortunately, I was at the tail end of the Boomers. By the time I was growing up, instead of formula, we were fed Tang.

We might call all this the "greener-faster-grass temptation." Some writers refer to it as the Hungry Ghost syndrome because it reveals the kind of gnawing spirit within us that can never be satiated. As the British-American theologian Mick Jagger put it: "I can't get no . . . satisfaction." We always wake up ravenous; we always try to stuff in more and more—but in the end we always go to sleep feeling a gnawing emptiness. Whatever we attach ourselves to, it is never enough.[12]

Of course, Jesus faced this sort of temptation himself in the wilderness. Satan (or the devil, depending on which Gospel you are reading) accosts Jesus in the desert, offering three temptations: turn stones to bread; dive off the temple; and take possession of the world's kingdoms and their power.[13] The psychology of the Tempter runs something like the following (and remember, Jesus is fully human—and he sits alone):

First, turn these stones to bread. You are fragile, vulnerable, dependent, and you're in the wilderness. Secure for yourself the goods you need! You never again need subject yourself to privation. Second, dive off the

---

12. See Rolheiser, *Forgotten Among the Lilies*, ix.

13. See Matthew 4:1–11 and Luke 4:1–13. I am using Matthew's ordering of the temptations; in Luke, the appearance of last two temptations are in reverse order.

temple and let the angels catch you. Right now, you are isolated and alienated from others, and you're in the wilderness. Give the crowd cause to adore you! You'll never feel rejected or abandoned again. Third, seize all the kingdoms of the world. Life is unpredictable, dangerous, and insecure—especially in the wilderness. Grab control; snatch power into your own hands; be your own god. Essentially, each of these three temptations boils down to a single temptation, the temptation to mistrust God. Satan entices: "Jesus, God has abandoned you. You are going to die out here. Your life will end up one big waste, a big nothing. And you are just sitting there passively. *Do* something to save yourself. Hurry up, before it's too late!" One senses the Devil's impatience. Or is it ours?

Every day, voices bellow to us, warning us that our wilderness life is not enough: not enough comfort, not enough love, not enough security; and, above all, God is not enough. Interestingly, Jesus responds in the same way to each of the devil's three wilderness temptations by quoting Scripture. "Time out," Jesus says, as if he were holding up his fingers in the shape of Rabbi Akiva's *bet*; "Let's see what God's Word says." Each time he responds, moreover, Jesus quotes from the Torah. In fact, he quotes from the same book of the Torah, Deuteronomy, from chapters 8–10, which describe how God faithfully maintains Israel in the wilderness. As the first biblical canonical unit, the Torah tells its audience what it means to be Israel. And the Torah ends with Deuteronomy, with Israel still standing on the wilderness side of the Jordan, looking across to the Promised Land, waiting. To be Israel thus means to wait. Slow down. Breathe. Wait. Trust that God will provide. Trust that God is enough. "Be still and know that I am God." It seems obvious that the opposite of rushing ourselves into distraction is slowing down in trust. "But I have calmed and quieted my soul, like a weaned child with its mother; my soul is like the weaned child that is with me. O Israel, hope in the Lord."[14] Recall the infamous South American hunting tribe that would periodically stop and make camp for apparently no reason. When asked why they kept pausing, their chief replied: "To let our souls catch up with us."[15] Israel's learning in the wilderness happened slowly—forty-years-slow—at about three miles per hour.[16]

But we have to admit that slowing down makes us uncomfortable. What if I come into the wilderness and I find only a threatening emptiness

14. Psalm 46:10; Psalm 131:2–3.

15. Muller, *Sabbath*, 70.

16. See Koyama, *Three Mile an Hour God*.

and desolation there? What if I find that I'm abandoned there, that I am Lost in the Cosmos? A professor friend of mine recently shared a metaphor that makes sense to me. He said that lately his life reminds him of traveling the Greek Islands. From one island, you can see the next; from that, another, and so on. Similarly, his life moved from one known achievement to the next: graduating from college, getting married, attending seminary, then on for the PhD. After earning his final degree, he and his wife had kids, moved to the first teaching job, bought a house, and began their careers: for him, his first book, tenure, and so on, until, finally, he got to the point where he could not see what was next. "One day, you're on an island looking out," he commented thoughtfully, "and you don't see any other islands—only open sea." For all of us, the image of the open sea represents the spiritual journey inward. This is a journey without clear boundaries, a scene which can trigger anxiety. Also, we grow anxious when we turn inward because we fear facing ourselves; like the friend of mine who said he contemplated leaving his wife and traveling to Russia, but then realized he would have to take himself along. At some point, we are all like Jacob at the stream, alone and silenced, wrestling with our past and with our inner demons. And this inner spiritual journey just keeps going further and deeper into the Open Sea of God.

Our inner journey slows us down, resisting any formula—so it can loom like a threatening void. My spiritual director puts it this way: "If your expectation fixes your attention on the Promised Land (some imagined highpoint you are aiming for—like some distant enchanted island), the desert (your ordinary, everyday life) will almost always disappoint you. But what happens, instead, if you bracket out in advance your demand to arrive at your fictional Promised Land? What if you let go of your wished for outcome from the outset?" The mantra here could read, "Determine NOT to determine; instead, simply notice." If we take the desert on its own terms—that is, ordinary everyday life—and if we look to see what really lay there, before ignoring or rejecting it, then perhaps we will find a beauty in the desert we could not otherwise imagine. What flowers grow in the desert? What sort of joy does the expansive desert sky invoke?

Chris Tomlin's butterflies surely must visit the desert on quiet days (see Figure 7, *Milkweed and Butterfly*). Tomlin is *The Saint John's Bible* illuminator who created the naturalist depictions of insects—insects all indigenous, by the way, either to Minnesota or to Wales, the two homesteads of those who collaborated on the project. Tomlin's illuminations prompt us to notice the ordinary, to pause and wonder and praise, as much with the dandelion as with the rose or rose-window. His butterflies float magnificently on the page. Yet Tomlin does not just include beautiful butterflies, but also mundane moths and daring dragonflies, and they are all stunning. Every common bug afire with God, we might suggest. Furthermore, it takes time to truly appreciate Tomlin's art. Otherwise, one might either pass by these insects as though they were mere wallpaper patterns, or nod to the butterflies, while ignoring the moths. We cannot rush a wildflower or an insect any more than we can rush a child growing up.

The life-cycle of the monarch depicted here symbolizes resurrection and rebirth, of course, but also it suggests a slow process of growth, beauty that takes time, that cannot be hurried. Notice the butterflies or dragonflies near you in the late summer and notice how they cannot be controlled. Their flight does not appear at all utilitarian, but more like some extravagant dance. They dart here and there like a kite in the wind. They have their own pace and agenda.

The same is true of spiritual formation. Thomas Merton once told a friend to stop trying so hard in prayer. Merton said: "'How does an apple ripen? It just sits in the sun.' A small green apple cannot ripen in one night by tightening its jaw in order to find itself the next morning miraculously large, red, ripe, and juicy."[17] In other words, apples unfold in God's time. Even so, our souls ripen much slower than at an apple's pace.

Let me put forth two more illuminations to ponder. The first one comes from the book of Judges (see Figure 3, *Judges Anthology*). At the bottom, a quote from that book reads: "All the people did what was right in their own eyes." What do you notice? What stands out in your mind? A certain beauty resonates from this illumination, but it is also shattered, and fragmented. Notice how it lacks unity, peace, stability, even a center. As we look closer we see that violence and frenzy runs throughout the illumination. The thin gold bars here are outweighed, as it were, by heavier black bars—the gold signifying the divine, the black representing human sin. Commenting on the gold wedges that illustrate God's continuing presence with his people, in spite of their frantic waywardness, illuminator Donald Jackson suggests the wedges are "sort of scurrying around, almost like divine sheep dogs, trying to pull all these people together, while they're all defying it, going their own way, and still surrounded by the symbols of their

---

17. Finley, *Merton's Palace of Nowhere*, 114.

yearning for foreign gods."[18] I facetiously think he should have added some cell phones to the illumination because this artwork signifies our modern frenetic mindset so well.

Contrast the art accompanying the book of Judges with this next one paired with the Jacob's ladder narrative from Genesis 28 (see Figure 4, *Jacob's Ladder*). What do you notice? In the biblical story, Jacob dreams and sees angels ascending and descending on a ladder between earth and heaven. Look at the angels. They float so free, as if in a dance. Spiritual formation always aims to set us free. Did you ever have a floating or flying dream? The freedom of the angels here reminds me of those dreams. Genesis mentions the angels "ascending and descending." I like that order. It is significant that ascending comes first. Why? Why do they ascend first? Because they already exist here, first. Angels camp all around us—right now—if we have eyes to see. "Surely, the Lord *IS* in this place and I did not know it," blurts Jacob after he wakes. *This* place, meaning potentially *any* place. And this place *now*. Although the ladder connects heaven and earth, the angels hardly seem to need it, do they? Evidently, this is not a two-story universe we are glimpsing, with the earthly down here and heavenly up there, or "out there," down some imagined time line to eternity. We find, instead, one, connected, spirit-infused realm, where all things hold sacramental value, at least potentially so. What about Chris Tomlin's butterfly wings interspersed throughout this Genesis illumination? Do they reveal divine presence? Is the illuminator suggesting that the holy—and the Holy One—shines out from all the ordinary objects around us? Tomlin's butterflies in *The Saint John's Bible* remind us that beauty becomes the ladder connecting heaven and earth. His butterflies remind us that beauty appears to us—un-conjured, often unbidden, surely UNRUSHED, alighting next to us at any given moment.

Bibliography

Berry, Wendell. *Hannah Coulter*. Berkeley: Counterpoint 2004.

Chesterton, G. K. *Manalive*. Collected Works of G. K. Chesterton 7. San Francisco: Ignatius, 2004.

Clement, Olivier. *Roots of Christian Mysticism*. New York: New City, 1996.

Finley, James. *Merton's Palace of Nowhere*. Notre Dame, IN: Ave Maria, 1978.

Koyama, Kosuke. *Three Mile an Hour God*. Maryknoll, NY: Orbis, 1979.

Kreeft, Peter. *Christianity for Modern Pagans*. San Francisco: Ignatius, 1993.

18. Sink, *The Art of the Saint John's Bible*, 53.

Lewis, C. S. *The Screwtape Letters*. 1942. Reprint, New York: HarperCollins, 2001.

———. *Letters to Malcom Chiefly on Prayer*. 1964. Reprint, San Diego: Harvest, 1973.

Muller, Wayne. *Sabbath: Finding Rest, Renewal, and Delight in Our Busy Lives*. New York: Bantam, 2000.

Rolheiser, Ronald. *Forgotten among the Lilies*. New York: Random House, 2005.

Saint John's Bible. Brother Alan Reed. https://www.youtube.com/watch?v=lK-bVPJyHKQ.

Sink, Susan. *The Art of* The Saint John's Bible: *The Complete Reader's Guide*. Collegeville, MN: Liturgical, 2013.

Twenty One Pilots. "Car Radio." *Regional at Best*. Self-published, 2011.

Walsh, Liam. *The New Yorker*, May 18, 2015. https://www.newyorker.com/magazine/2015/05/18/.

5

The Marginal Life of Manuscripts

What *The Saint John's Bible* Teaches Us through Error

JACK R. BAKER

IN HIS PLAY *THE ROCK*, T. S. Eliot contemplates the nature of the modern world as shaped by the industrial mind:

> The endless cycle of idea and action,
>
> Endless invention, endless experiment,
>
> Brings knowledge of motion, but not of stillness;
>
> Knowledge of speech, but not of silence;
>
> Knowledge of words, and ignorance of the Word.
>
> All our knowledge brings us nearer to death,
>
> But nearness to death no nearer to God.
>
> Where is the Life we have lost in living?
>
> Where is the wisdom we have lost in knowledge?
>
> Where is the knowledge we have lost in information?
>
> The cycles of Heaven in twenty centuries
>
> Brings us farther from God and nearer to the Dust.[1]

As a professor of literature trained in medieval studies, these questions resonate with me in profound ways—I care a great deal about the character of

---

1. Eliot, *The Waste Land and Other Poems*, 81.

59

ancient books in a world that doesn't have much time for them. And I am moved by the thought that there is a goodness we lose in modern books. I am, of course, not interested in vilifying modern printing, which is a bit like biting the hand that feeds me. But there is something to be said about how medieval manuscripts differ from modern books in what they offer to us, the readers. I hope to say that something in the pages that follow.

Each medieval manuscript is a culture unto itself. A manuscript is given a shelf-mark (a unique name and number identifier particular to the library in which it is housed) so that we can identify where it lives; it has a provenance; it is written in a datable and locatable script; its text resides on animal skins that once roamed medieval countrysides.

Manuscripts are living objects whose great value grows as they age. Thus, we treat ancient manuscripts with the utmost care, hoping to preserve them for the ages to come just as they have been so lovingly preserved for us. Yet, if you spend any time with a medieval manuscript, you will quickly be surprised to see the margins of these precious handiworks populated with sundry scribbles, jottings, doodlings, and writings. It is as if the margins of medieval manuscripts are teeming with a vibrant life—one that flourishes on the outskirts of the carefully ruled margins of the primary text.

These margins have served as spaces for scribes, copyists, commentators, students, and children to gather over the ages, contributing their voices to the pages through the words and images they placed in the empty spaces enfolding the text.[2] Given that the medievals were so comfortable populating the margins of costly manuscripts with often crude, juvenile, and irreverent sketches, we might conclude that their textual decorum was a bit lax; imagine today what would happen if someone were to borrow the *Lindisfarne Gospels* manuscript (Cotton Nero D IV) from the British Library, adding to the margins his own drawing of a knight fighting a snail.

But the marginal inhabitants of manuscript pages are often also instructive—from them we learn much about the medievals whose hands touched the careworn vellum across the long centuries. We learn that they had clever senses of humor, that they sometimes needed help from glosses (words written in one's native tongue next to obscure foreign words) to read a Latin text, and that they would occasionally make glaring errors that required correction.

2. For the role children have played in filling the margins of manuscripts through the ages, see Lerer's fascinating article "Devotion and Defacement," 126–53.

And it is in this marginal life of medieval manuscripts that we might also learn about ourselves. We learn that we have lost a certain knowledge about ourselves because we have come to treat books as static objects, as artifacts. Perhaps this book-as-artifact mentality is owing to modern print culture. With the advent of the printing press in the fifteenth century, the Western world began its quick-tempoed march toward textual standardization and mass production. And if we know anything about textual technologies, then we know that with each new technology, something is lost and something is gained. So what is the knowledge we have lost and gained as we moved from a manuscript culture to a book culture? Importantly, books were no longer the prerogative of only the church and the wealthy. The printing press became a great social equalizer as texts became affordable to many who did not possess the wealth required to own a manuscript. In fact, the history of the Bible and its movement into vernacular languages occurs alongside this technology. And though there is much more we have gained from this technology, there is also much we have lost. The loss I am interested in here is the life of those things that live in the margins of manuscript pages—the marginalia. Though we have lost marginalia in modern books, we do have footnotes and endnotes—perhaps the modern equivalent of marginalia. Throughout this essay, then, I'll be placing my own marginalia in the space at the bottom of the page. Some of this marginalia is scholarly, some bawdy, some commentary, some tomfoolery, but all of it is part of the character of this essay, which takes itself seriously even if its footnotes, at times, do not.

It is ironic that we often treat modern texts with greater reverence than it appears medievals did with their manuscripts. But perhaps we don't often create in the margins of our books because we aren't invested in them like the medievals were in their manuscripts. After all, the word *manuscript* means 'handwritten,' and so its name reveals how it was shaped. A thing that is handwritten requires careful planning, collaboration among artists and scribes, and a considerable amount of time and wealth to complete. Manuscripts have histories because they have long lives. They were created by people for others and for God, to be read, to be loved, to be shared, to be cherished. They are snapshots into the past. They are local and particular. They have changed lives, crowned kings, converted sinners, and inspired dreamers. Perhaps it is this very living nature of manuscripts that invited participants to fill their margins.

By contrast, each modern book exists in many identical copies, the only distinguishing character being that which we might add to its pages with our own hands. But each medieval manuscript, even if a copy (called 'witnesses' because they testify to the original text) is unique.[3] It is a virtue of a modern book to be clean, neat, and identical in every copy. It is a virtue of a manuscript to be a living creature. Our modern sensibilities don't like messy texts that have been written on or doodled in.[4] In fact, rather than existing as a sign of a book's living identity, marginal scribblings, doodlings, and notes—not to say anything about the occasional printed textual error—become a sign of a book's imperfection, its inefficiency, its human error.[5] And so we might say that modern books, in many ways, have lost their individual, living nature.[6]

Indeed, for a book to make it to print today with even a handful of errors would be a sign of its poor construction. Too many of those errors in a book and an inattentive editor is out of work.[7] Even those errors that occasionally

3. Readers interested in a detailed, colorful, and instructive introduction to manuscript studies, see Clemens and Graham, *Introduction to Manuscript Studies*. For those curious about the history of medieval scripts, see Drogin, *Medieval Calligraphy*.

4. You know that feeling when you have bought a copy from an online bookseller that claims it is *lightly* marked up only to receive what must have been a copy owned by a preschooler who was left alone with a highlighter and his repressed rage over a snack time that consisted of celery and raisins.

5. When was the last time you thought of a modern book as a living thing? When was the last time the margins of a modern book called out to you to populate their emptiness with the musings of your imagination? For most of us, the last time we felt free to fill the margins of books was in grade-school. You too may yet recall the halcyon days of our youth when we leafed through our school-assigned textbook to see what gems lay hidden inside, the history of the long line of previous owners—a signature, a doodle, a funny-to-only-12-year-olds comment furtively penned when Mrs. Hannigan had her back to the class. Or maybe it was your junior-high year book, the one in which Jimmy Current scrawled on its spine the oh-so-original "I signed your crack" (the sort of humor the medievals would certainly have appreciated).

6. That is not to say all modern books that have been written on are these sorts—you may in fact own a modern book that is precious to you for any number of reasons. A grandmother's bible, a Winnie the Pooh book you read to your daughter throughout her childhood, a heavily annotated text you've taught from for over twenty years. These are books you'd run into a burning house to save. If you can imagine such a book, then you can begin to understand just how precious medieval manuscripts were—and perhaps just how odd it is to us that such manuscripts would be written on in such a way.

7. *The Wicked Bible* is an early example of the dangers of print errors and the speed at which errors could be remedied. The Ten Commandments (Exodus 20:14) in this 1631 bible commanded readers: "Thou shalt Commit adultery." The consequences were severe, and the London publishers lost their license to print. No fear of such far reaching

do find their way into print are easily removed by the second printing. Not unlike our own word-processed work, a textual error is amended quickly and quietly, leaving behind no trail of its waywardness.

Within this context, errors and marginalia are wanderings; they distract; they reveal missteps; they are often occasions for ridicule; they stir our imaginations; they demonstrate our fallibility—and there are few things we can tolerate less than others seeing our mistakes. But what if our mistakes were soaked into the skins of calves and not so easily removed? What if they were trapped beneath the gold-foil of an illuminated roundel? What if they were captured on the costly pages of a modern manuscript that took over 15 years to bring to fruition? And what if an error-free text was no longer an option, or even the ideal?

In the remainder of this essay, I examine several marginal-meanderings and errata left behind in a few medieval manuscripts and one modern manuscript: *The Saint John's Bible*. I am particularly interested in imagining marginal citizens and textual emendations as gifts to posterity. They are gifts that bless us with the hope of goodness even in slowness, impermanence, and imperfection.[8]

Marginalia: The Life of Manuscript Margins

For ages readers have been enamored with the spaces around a page's text. We are drawn to them—they call out to us to fill them with the thoughts and images dancing in our minds. Herman Melville once wrote that "the best reading was on the fly leaves," those blank pages at the beginning or end of a work, and in 1890 the American painter William Morris Hunt poignantly observed that "[t]here is scarcely a child whose first impulse is not to scribble on the wall or any fresh piece of paper." What is it with us and blank spaces? Why do they impress upon us a sense of incompleteness rather than completeness? Hunt is right, though—we gravitate toward the edges of a page from a young age: "The child's scribbling on the margin of his schoolbooks is really worth more to him than all he gets out of them. To him the

---

consequences with a manuscript—a simple emendation would suffice.

8. Anytime we offer a reading, we become interpreters: "A reading is an interpretation from a position—a story told from a vantage point—and often the specific object of study has been chosen because it enables the interpreter to broach an issue of broader significance for the study of visual materials." Sears and Thomas, eds. *Reading Medieval Images*, 1–2.

margin is the best part of all books, and he finds in it the soothing influence of a clear sky in a landscape."[9] While I certainly wouldn't agree with Hunt's dim view of what we might get out of a book's actual text, I do find myself agreeing with the sentiment that a book's margins are spaces imbued with potential—spaces in which creativity might flourish.

In life, when we give ourselves margin, we leave room for the unplanned and unexpected, for error and correction. Manuscript margins are like this, not only because they provide us with room to work through error, but also because they give us room in which to offer a reading, a commentary, or an annotation.

In his poem "Marginalia," Billy Collins touches upon the active life of blank spaces around a text, expressing that space's power to inspire the imagination:

> We have all seized the white perimeter as our own
>
> and reached for a pen if only to show
>
> we did not just laze in an armchair turning pages;
>
> we pressed a thought into the wayside,
>
> planted an impression along the verge.[10]

These impressions we plant "along the verge" propel us both backward and forward in time. As we add our own comments to the margins of our modern books, we take part in the ancient practice of speaking with and into the text—we join our voice to the voices of those who have gone before us, for those who will come after us. We become, in Collins's words, time-travelers:

> Even Irish monks in their cold scriptoria
>
> jotted along the borders of the Gospels
>
> brief asides about the pains of copying,
>
> a bird singing near their window,
>
> or the sunlight that illuminated their page—
>
> anonymous men catching a ride into the future
>
> on a vessel more lasting than themselves.

Some of the scribes and readers who caught "a ride into the future" on their manuscript-vessels would have been a hoot to have at a cocktail party.

9. These quotes are taken from Lerer, "Devotion and Defacement," 126.

10. Collins, "Marginalia," 249–51.

Have you seen some of the things they have added to the margins of their manuscripts? If we could visit them and come back to the future, I wonder what stories we'd tell. Perhaps this is one of the lasting virtues of scholarship in manuscript studies—we get to travel to the past so that we might bring meaning back to the future. As his recent work, *Meetings with Remarkable Manuscripts: Twelve Journeys into the Medieval World*, demonstrates, we should be thankful for scholars like Christopher de Hamel who do such time-travel work for us.[11]

The most audacious scribblers are the ones I'd corner first at the party. One of the oddest and most enduring characteristics of certain medieval illuminated manuscripts are the drolleries (or grotesques) that live in their margins. Commonly found in manuscripts from the 13th-15th centuries, drolleries are a type of marginalia depicting grotesque, hybrid creatures. Many of them are humorous, and some of them are ribald, so you'd better know your audience well before sharing any with them. The modern reader of manuscripts often wonders at the fact that such images live in such close juxtaposition to devotional religious texts. Certainly the irony was not lost on readers across the ages. But what to do with violent, pooping monkeys? A common drollery, the anthropomorphized monkeys sometimes wield weapons; they sometimes wield feces; but, nearly every time, they wreak havoc on the page.[12]

But it is not like monkeys have the corner on the market of lunatic, personified animals. Do you remember the scene in *Monty Python and the Holy Grail* when Arthur and his knights are led by Tim the Enchanter to the lair of the Killer Rabbit of Caerbannog? Even though Tim warns them that it is "no ordinary rabbit!," they foolishly approach and lose many fine knights to the hellish creature's onslaught. The blokes in Monty Python had done their research, because murder-minded rabbits were all the rave in medieval marginalia.

Why do these rabbits proliferate in manuscript margins like they do in the wild? Because rabbits were, in their real lives, copiously copulating creatures, their lives in the margins of manuscripts reflected such. Their presence on the page came to indicate innocence, cowardice, even passive

---

11. De Hamel, *Meetings with Remarkable Manuscripts*.

12. Let me say, every time I see these edge-bound-creatures, I feel like I've stumbled upon some class bully's textbook where, bored with a lecture, he's decided to transform his teachers into poop-wielding primates. If you're interested in the rather ribald marginalia, Carl S. Pyrdum, III has compiled a great number of these at his blog, http://www.gotmedieval.com.

but willing sexuality. And, as much as we find it funny today, medieval artists likewise found humor in the prospect of rabbits inverting hierarchy, getting their revenge, and taking over the world. So when you see a colony of rabbits besieging a castle in a manuscript, listen to the voices from the past and give thanks that you've not yet crossed these killers from the family *Leporidae*.

As it is with rabbits and monkeys, so it is with a good deal of the marginalia we encounter in manuscripts—we feel a bit like we've walked into a room just as someone delivers the punchline of a fantastic joke. We really have no idea why the joke was funny, but we feel obliged to laugh. The "Knight and Snail" motif is one of these jokes that is told time and again in the margins of texts. Though prevalent, the motif's meaning remains ambiguous and malleable. As art historian Michael Camille notes in *Image on the Edge: The Margins of Medieval Art*:

> Just as [a] proverb has no single divine authority, but is spoken in response to specific situations, marginal imagery likewise lacks the iconographic stability of a religious narrative or icon. The knight and snail motif is . . . ready to be placed into a variety of contexts, where it will work in different ways and mean different things. The medieval artist's ability was measured not in terms of invention, as today, but in the capacity to combine traditional motifs in new and challenging ways.[13]

Knights and snails, rabbits, and monkeys, become local and particular to the manuscripts in which they appear, and so their meaning is often contextual.

So if there are many different ways to read medieval marginalia, is meaning elusive? Well, it may be elusive as a hare, but it is certainly there, even if it is at times a bit juvenile—even if that meaning really only made sense for a particular reader in a particular place. But our modern sensibilities at times betray us. We want to read things into medieval marginalia that fit our own research agendas; for instance, "Meyer Schapiro, writing under the influence of psychoanalytical theory in the 1930s, saw marginal images as the liberation of unconscious impulses repressed by religion,

---

13. Camille, *Image on the Edge*, 36. If ever a children's toy line of battle snails hits the market, we'll have the medievals to thank. To read about battle snails, see Randall, "The Snail in Gothic Marginal Warfare," 358–67.

while, more recently, one scholar has described them as 'like the doodles in student notebooks today . . . the signs of daydreams.'"[14]

But as Camille argues, we ought not think in such binary terms, categorizing marginalia as either simply "free associations" or the embodiment of repression. Because medieval manuscripts were local and particular—that is, they were typically created for a particular patron or community who existed in a specific locale at a particular time in history—we must often work hard to reconstruct the meaning of their marginalia. For instance, scholars have learned that the motif of the knight and snail, though odd to us, could have signified several things to the manuscript's original community: an erotic encounter, the vice of cowardice which was seen as a sin against God, or a common proverbial expression like "to flee a snail."[15]

Errata: The Gift in Error

Though marginalia such as drolleries and personified fauna are all the rave in medieval manuscripts, they are not the only inhabitants of these spaces. What is more, a good number of margin-dwellers tend not to be flourishes of profound creativity. Some are mostly utilitarian. Yet, even ostensibly utilitarian marginalia are beautifully instructive. I am thinking here of marginalia like textual emendations, glosses, commentaries, and corrections.

Errata are common among the tightly-penned script of medieval manuscripts.[16] And since it is a consequence of a manuscript page's frugal economy that there is, quite literally, no room for error in the body of the text, scribes often found themselves inventing clever methods for correcting their mistakes. What is a scribe to do, say, when he skips a line because two lines begin the same way (we call this an eyeskip)? What if he introduces an error into the text? It cannot simply be erased like graphite from paper or pixels from a screen. Erasure was a risk for any scribe since it entailed scraping both flesh and ink from the page with his penknife. Depending upon how long the ink had set, the process of erasure could thin the page. And if the scribe himself never notices his error, the correction is left for readers to make in the margins.

If you can imagine the amount of time that went into a single recto (or right-hand page of an open book) of a manuscript, you begin to understand

14. Ibid.

15. Ibid., 35–36.

16. *Errata* is a black-tie Latin word for "you done messed up A-Æthelred!"

how easy it must have been for scribes to become exhausted and thus prone to error. You might inversely marvel at the fact that, given the tedious nature of such work, there aren't more errors in medieval manuscripts. From the tenth century onward, it was common for scribes and readers who caught an error to place a correction or supply a missing line in the margin. The text and margin were then linked by a pair of matching signs, which paleographers call *signes-de-renvoi*, or 'signs of return'. These signs took on many different (and often decorative) forms. For the manuscript page that bears the rather frequent errors of a less than competent scribe, such 'returns' were particularly helpful because they allowed for several different symbols to be used, helping the reader avoid confusion.

One utilitarian marginalia I particularly like is the *manicula*, or 'little hand'. "From the later thirteenth century onward," it was common for scribes "to enter in the margin a sketch of a hand with the index finger extended to point toward the beginning of the significant passage."[17] Shaped like the large foam fingers we see today at most sporting events in the United States, these considerably less obnoxious little hands draw our attention to the margin, only to point us back to the text itself so that we might focus on certain words.

An Error in *The Bible of St. Louis*

The slowness manuscripts require of us is refreshing to this modern reader. When I spend time with a manuscript, I am struck by how often I find myself moving between the primary text and the margins because the two give life to each other. I've often told my students that slowness rewards the careful reader. I try to help them practice such slowness. In one of my literature courses we spend nearly an entire class on two paragraphs of Marilynne Robinson's *Gilead*, a moving passage in which John Ames imagines how baseball and listening to a parishioner unburden the weight of grief are alike, both revealing the strength and beauty of human energy as it moves between people who are in a space together—"the loveliness is just in that presence."[18] But I haven't always practiced what I preach; manuscripts had to teach me how to practice slowness in their presence.

As an intimidated student at a difficult graduate program in medieval studies, I felt inferior to many of my classmates who always seemed leaps

17. Clemens and Graham, *Introduction to Manuscript Studies*, 44.
18. Robinson, *Gilead*, 51.

and bounds ahead of where I was intellectually. In my first summer of the program, I enrolled in "Reading Medieval Images," falling in love with medieval manuscripts. And so, when I set off to write one of my first seminar papers as a graduate student, I *tried* to hit a home run.

My essay was concerned with an error in the illumination of an early thirteenth-century manuscript called *The Bible of St. Louis*.[19] This bible was among several popular picture-bible manuscripts of the thirteenth to fifteenth centuries, called *Bibles moralisées*—or *moralized bibles*. These bibles

19. *Biblia de San Luis.* Vol. 1.

were quite exquisite, staggeringly expensive, heavily illustrated, stunningly illuminated; they are exemplars of the interplay between signification, interpretation, and how the visual experience of a thing shapes our faith. Each page of these bibles was covered with images accompanying a biblical text and its interpretation.

When our class was given the chance to thumb through a fine art re-production of *The Bible of St. Louis*, my imagination was stirred by a series of images on the verso (or left-hand page of an open book) of the fifth page in the first volume. On that page is depicted the creation of humans as recorded in Genesis 1:26. On the lower right quadrant of that page is a pruned quotation of the Latin text of Genesis 2:10: "*Fluuius egrediebatur ad irrigandum paradisum qui diuiditur in quatuor capita*" [A river went out to water paradise, which is divided into four]. Below this text and image is its moralization: "*Quatuor capita fluuii paradisi significant IIIIor maiores uir-tutes sicilicet prudentiam, temperantiam, fortitudinem, iusticiam de quibus sancta ecclesia adimpletur*" [The four heads of the river of paradise signify the four principal virtues, which are prudence, temperance, fortitude, [and] justice, of which the holy church is full].[20]

In the adjoining roundel are five figures within a roofed structure; four of the figures are the personified virtues, Ladies Prudence, Temperance, Fortitude, and Justice. They are seated around a larger, standing woman, Lady Ecclesia, who is holding a chalice. Three of these women hold a small disk on which is depicted an icon traditionally associated with her virtue— the fourth, Lady Justice, holds a sword. In following tradition, the artist has placed a prowling lion in Lady Fortitude's disk and a kneeling camel in Lady Temperance's. However, Lady Prudence, whose icon commonly is a snake (often coiled around a staff), is holding a disk with a bird in the midst of flames, which is clearly a phoenix.[21] The phoenix, however, is tradition-ally a symbol of resurrection or chastity, not prudence.[22] The artist seems to have introduced an error into a visually stunning manuscript.

20. The Latin text of the moralization can be traced to St. Ambrose who, borrowing his ideas from Plato, introduces the fourth-century Christian west to the cardinal virtues by harmonizing them with Genesis 2:10. See Plato, *The Republic*, 4:433 and Ambrose, *Patrologia Latina*, 14:280.

21. For an in depth study of the representations of virtues in thirteenth-century France, see Male, *Religious Art in France*, 99–133. See also Katzenellenbogen, *Allegories of the Virtues and Vices in Medieval Art*, 75–84. In his study, Male notes that "[a] bird surrounded by flames can only be the phoenix" (119).

22. For an analysis of the animals on the discs, Katzenellenbogen offers a reading of

In my essay I floated a number of theories for how such an error could have made its way into the manuscript—at that point in my studies I still thought scholarship meant proving I was right. Perhaps an artist who worked in the scriptorium where *The Bible of St. Louis* was made fell asleep during what was supposed to be a quick lunch, rushed out the door and down the street to Notre Dame de Paris to complete preliminary sketches of his virtues that were to be patterned after the virtue and vice cycle carved into its stone, and did shoddy work. Perhaps the artist was illiterate, or, at any rate, unable to read Latin and so did his best to assign icons to virtues— three out of four is not too bad.

The reason I've written this essay is because my experience with *The Bible of St. Louis* is bittersweet to me. It is the spark that lit the flame of manuscript studies that burns bright in me today; yet, it is also an abiding source of embarrassment for me. But more importantly, it is one of the rather formative moments in my life as a student. The seminar paper I wrote on the error in this bible was a disaster. It was just terrible. I imagined my professors sitting around the long table in the Rawlinson Center, each reading it aloud amidst the incredulous chortles of colleagues. As I look back at my writing (I still have the paper!) I am ashamed of the stilted nature of my prose, the simplistic syntax, the near absence of a thesis, the confident conclusions I drew given the tenuous nature of my evidence.

The graduate seminar paper, like a medieval manuscript, is a document unto itself—one that requires certain knowledge of its form and its content. I was given a chance to rewrite and correct my shabby work, and so I learned from my error. I don't think my revised essay was much better, but I am certain the process of erring and correcting was instrumental in my becoming a better writer and person. And I am thankful for the gift of Dr. Teviotdale's kindness and instruction—by them she taught me slowness and discernment in my writing. What is more, she opened my eyes to the margins and errors of medieval manuscripts. And because I had a professor who was willing to hold me accountable to a high standard and to direct me toward improvement, I did not give up on manuscripts. In fact, my first publication was a transcription and translation of a Latin charm against thieves in a Cambridge University manuscript.[23]

"The Virtue and Vice Cycle of Notre-Dame," (76). Here he identifies Prudence holding a disk with a serpent and Chastity holding a disk with a phoenix.

23. Baker, "Christ's Crucifixion and Robin Hood and the Monk," 71–85.

Margin and Error in *The Saint John's Bible*

My scholarly work with manuscripts brings me joy. So when the Spring Arbor University community had the opportunity to host a high-quality art reproduction of one volume of *The Saint John's Bible* during the 2015–16 academic year, I was understandably thrilled. We had the profound joy of housing in White Library the Heritage Edition of "The Gospel and Acts."[24]

Though the collaborators of *The Saint John's Bible* strictly adhered to ancient techniques of manuscript production, they differed from their medieval counterparts in final intent; unlike medieval manuscripts, the life after birth for *The Saint John's Bible* was to be lived among the people. What is more, it was created using traditional methods and materials while engaging contemporary questions and concerns; and so, it is the culmination of a community of artists, scholars, and theologians and is a modern exemplar of how we might create beautiful things by returning to practices that by modern standards are slow, impermanent, and imperfect.

In our time with *The Saint John's Bible*, I came to learn that it differs from medieval manuscripts in an important way: unlike the at times confusing nature of the imagery in ancient texts, *The Saint John's Bible* is contemporary, and thus we struggle less to understand the images that populate its pages and margins. Because of its contemporary nature, it is also able to teach us about the local and particular nature of the *The Saint John's Bible* and its community of artists. They are not nameless scribes and illustrators, forgotten to those who come after. In fact, a companion book has been published, elucidating the richness and depth of meaning in the art of the bible.[25] The contemporary nature of the images on the page, along with a book explaining them, sets *The Saint John's Bible* apart and locates it precisely in a tradition and time and place.

Yet, it is not so unlike a medieval manuscript: *The Saint John's Bible* is alive with marginalia . . . and errata. Among the seven volumes of the bible the pages brim full with the flora and fauna of Minnesota and Wales—the two communities across the world that shaped the project; and there are also several errors that have crept into the pages of this costly work of art. But it is what those working on *The Saint John's Bible* decided to do after errors were introduced into the manuscript that is particularly instructive.

---

24. https://www.saintjohnsbible.org/promotions/heritage.
25. Sink, *The Art of The Saint John's Bible.*

This first error to make its way into *The Saint John's Bible* occurred in Mark 3:20, near the *Sower and the Seed* illumination. As Susan Sink tells us, when the error was discovered, "the idea of the 'line of return' was established to point to the place where the line should go."[26] But here the artists and scribes made a profound, not simply utilitarian, decision: The errors would not only be conspicuous, they would be made meaningful. And so, we observe the bird in the left margin of the page pulling by a cord—and with some great labor one imagines—the missing scripture. However, this auspicious[27] assistant's work is not yet done, for it appears to have flown over to the illumination in the right-hand column of the page to feed on the golden seeds (the Word) that the Sower has sown. Thus, the bird who has wings not only restores the Word, but also consumes and spreads it. How much more work is there for us who have ears to hear and listen?

When a scribe omitted a line in 2 *Chronicles*, the artists transformed the error into a moment of beauty. The return was accomplished by making a home for a lemur in the right margin of the page, just above the marginal gloss "or baboons"; the ring-tailed lemur from Madagascar hangs from a vine with his right hand, pointing us to where the missing text belongs in the column. With his left hand and both feet, he is pulling up the omitted line. Desiring to uncover a profound reason for the baboon's presence in the margin, I wrote Fr. Michael Patella, who kindly wrote back to inform me that sometimes, a baboon is just a baboon. We can, I think, still be moved by the active, living creature who is performing the work of restoring scripture to its rightful place in line.

Perhaps my favorite creature living in the margins of *The Saint John's Bible* is the clever bumblebee in Wisdom 7 (see Figure 5, *Bee Error Treatment*). As Susan Sink tells us, "[o]ver the course of the project, each of the scribes made an error in the text that could not be erased." Often such omissions "seemed striking in their importance;" e.g., in this passage the scribes omitted the line "I called on God, and the spirit of wisdom came to me." And so the bumblebee working a da Vinci contraption was given life.[28] Such a contraption, built with pulleys and cords, allows the bumblebee to perform a great work of heavy lifting—the sort of heavy

---

26. Ibid., 232.

27. The etymology of this word is worth a trip to the *OED* to appreciate my pun here.

28. Ibid., 133.

lifting these splendid creatures play in engineering the pollination and flourishing of plant life in our world.

Rather than removing errors from *The Saint John's Bible*, those invested in its high quality chose to leave them there as a sign of the living nature of the bible. The errors are a testament to the human touch that helped bring it to fruition. They are gifts to those living and those yet to come. They instruct us to come to terms with human limits, to acknowledge our fallibility, and to creatively approach our errors so that, out of their ruin, we might cultivate goodness and beauty.

We humans are fairly predictable. When we stumble, we look around to make sure no one saw us. When we sing out of key, we hope everyone around us is loud enough to drown us out. When we make mistakes, we are tempted to cover them up, to hide them. But if we follow the example of those who worked on *The Saint John's Bible*, we come to know that the life that lacks margins is one that has no room to attend to and learn from error.

Conclusion

The not-yet-completeness of manuscripts calls to mind our not-yet-completeness as people who live in a redeemed world that still anticipates Christ's return. As I write this on the first Sunday of Advent, these words are particularly poignant.

Manuscripts teach us that our endeavors in this life, no matter how grand, will always be marked by their incompleteness. They teach us that if we practice slowness, acknowledge our impermanence, and recognize our errancy, we may find blessing. To embrace our tendency to wander does not mean we accept things as they are—it means we accept a posture of humility and thankfulness: humility, because out of our error might come goodness; thankfulness, because we live in the hope of Christ who is our completeness.

It is my hope that my own meanderings through manuscript marginalia and errata might encourage the reader to imagine how something as small as the margins of medieval manuscripts can be strange places where we might gather and find knowledge not of motion, but of stillness, not of speech, but of silence, and not of words alone, but of the infallible Word. *The Saint John's Bible* will stand for ages to come as a modern-medieval manuscript—an exemplar of human achievement for the glory of God. And perhaps the life of its margins and errata—the marks of true craftsmanship—will inspire its readers too. May our lives be like the pages of a medieval manuscript—with enough margin to be filled with humor, only occasionally marked by error, and more often than not inspired by the hope of correction.

Bibliography

Ambrose, Saint. *Patrologia Latina*. Vol. 14. Edited by J. P. Migne. Paris: Migne, 1845.

Baker, Jack R. "Christ's Crucifixion and Robin Hood and the Monk: A Latin Charm against Thieves in Cambridge, University Library MS Ff.5.48." *Transactions of the Cambridge Bibliographical Society* 14 (2010) 71–85.

Bovey, Alixe. *Monsters and Grotesques in Medieval Manuscripts*. Toronto: University of Toronto Press, 2002.

Camille, Michael. *Image on the Edge: The Margins of Medieval Art*. London: Reaktion, 2004.

Clemens, Raymond, and Timothy Graham. *Introduction to Manuscript Studies*. Ithaca, NY: Cornell University Press, 2007.

Collins, Billy. "Marginalia." *Poetry*, February 1996, 249–51.

Drogin, Marc. *Medieval Calligraphy: Its History and Technique*. New York: Dover, 1989.

Eliot, T. S. *The Waste Land and Other Poems*. New York: Houghton Mifflin Harcourt, 2014.

Hamel, Christopher de. *Meetings with Remarkable Manuscripts: Twelve Journeys into the Medieval World*. New York: Penguin, 2017.

Katzenellenbogen, Adolf. *Allegories of the Virtues and Vices in Medieval Art*. 2nd ed. Toronto: University of Toronto Press, 1989.

Lerer, Seth. "Devotion and Defacement: Reading Children's Marginalia." *Representations* 118.1 (2012) 126–53.

Mâle, Emile. *Religious Art in France: The Late Middle Ages—A Study of Medieval Iconography and Its Sources*. Edited by Harry Bober. Princeton: Princeton University Press, 1987.

Plato. *Plato: The Republic, Books 1–5*. Translated by Paul Shorey. Rev. ed. Loeb Classical Library. Cambridge: Harvard University Press, 1930.

Randall, Lilian M. C. "The Snail in Gothic Marginal Warfare." *Speculum* 37.3 (1962) 358–67.

Robinson, Marilynne. *Gilead: A Novel*. 2004. Reprint ed. New York: Picador, 2006.

Sears, Elizabeth Langsford, and Thelma Katrina Thomas, eds. *Reading Medieval Images: The Art Historian and the Object*. Ann Arbor: University of Michigan Press, 2002.

Sink, Susan. *The Art of The Saint John's Bible: The Complete Reader's Guide*. Collegeville, MN: The Saint John's Bible, 2013.

Figure 1: *Creation*, Donald Jackson with
contributions from Chris Tomlin.

76

Figure 2: *Ten Commandments*, Thomas Ingmire.

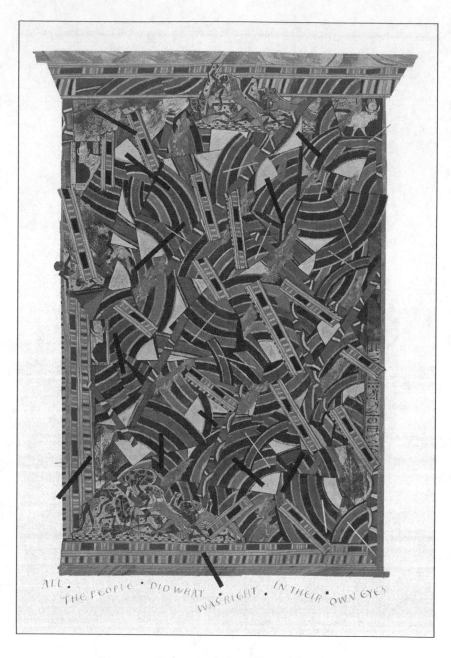

Figure 3: *Judges Anthology*, Donald Jackson.

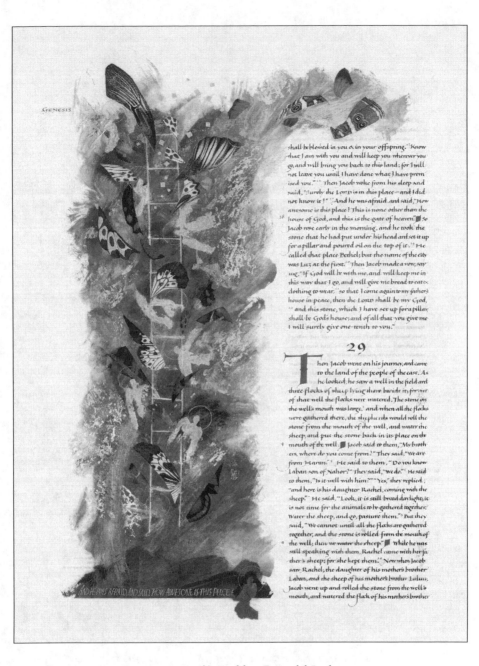

Figure 4: *Jacob's Ladder*, Donald Jackson
with contributions from Chris Tomlin.

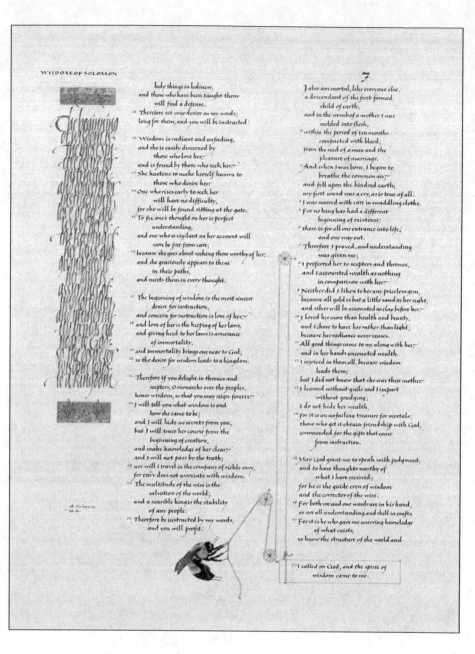

Figure 5: *Bee Error Treatment,* Chris Tomlin;
scribe: Sally Mae Joseph.

Figure 6: *Transfiguration*, Donald Jackson
with contributions from Aidan Hart.

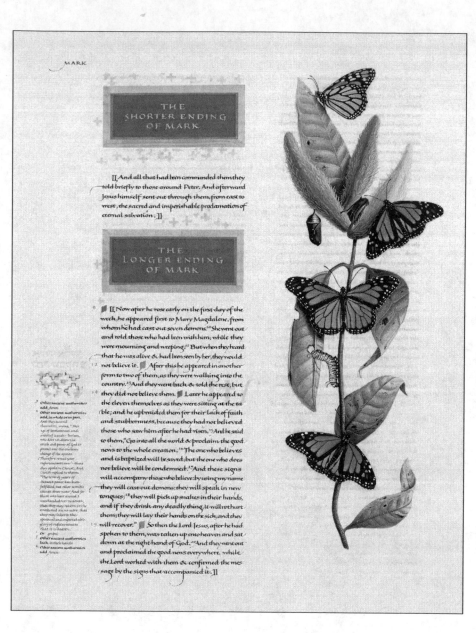

THE
SHORTER ENDING
OF MARK

[[And all that had been commanded them they
told briefly to those around Peter. And afterward
Jesus himself sent out through them, from east to
west, the sacred and imperishable proclamation of
eternal salvation.]]

THE
LONGER ENDING
OF MARK

⁹ [[Now after he rose early on the first day of the
week, he appeared first to Mary Magdalene, from
whom he had cast out seven demons.¹⁰ She went out
and told those who had been with him, while they
were mourning and weeping.¹¹ But when they heard
that he was alive & had been seen by her, they would
not believe it. ¹² After this he appeared in another
form to two of them, as they were walking into the
country.¹³ And they went back & told the rest, but
they did not believe them. ¹⁴ Later he appeared to
the eleven themselves as they were sitting at the table; and he upbraided them for their lack of faith
and stubbornness, because they had not believed
those who saw him after he had risen.¹⁵ And he said
to them, "Go into all the world & proclaim the good
news to the whole creation.¹⁶ The one who believes
and is baptized will be saved; but the one who does
not believe will be condemned.¹⁷ And these signs
will accompany those who believe: by using my name
they will cast out demons; they will speak in new
tongues;¹⁸ they will pick up snakes in their hands,
and if they drink any deadly thing, it will not hurt
them; they will lay their hands on the sick, and they
will recover." ¹⁹ So then the Lord Jesus, after he had
spoken to them, was taken up into heaven and sat
down at the right hand of God.²⁰ And they went out
and proclaimed the good news everywhere, while
the Lord worked with them & confirmed the message by the signs that accompanied it.]]

*ᵇ Other ancient authorities
add *Amen.
*ᶜ Other ancient authorities
add, in whole or in part,
And they excused
themselves, saying, "This
age of lawlessness and
unbelief is under Satan,
who does not allow the
truth and power of God to
prevail over the unclean
things of the spirits.
Therefore reveal your
righteousness now"—those
they spoke to Christ. And
Christ replied to them,
"The term of years of
Satan's power has been
fulfilled, but other terrible
things draw near." And for
those who have sinned I
was handed over to death,
that they may return to the
truth and sin no more, that
they may inherit the
spiritual and imperishable
glory of righteousness
that is in heaven.
*ᵈ Or gospel
*ᵉ Other ancient authorities
lack, in their hands
*ᶠ Other ancient authorities
add Amen.

Figure 7: *Milkweed and Butterfly*, Chris Tomlin.

Figure 8: *Luke Anthology*, Donald Jackson with contributions from Aidan Hart and Sally Mae Joseph.

Figure 9: *Crucifixion*, Donald Jackson.

Figure 10: *I Am Sayings*, Thomas Ingmire.

Figure 11: *Resurrection*, Donald Jackson.

Figure 12: *Pentecost*, Donald Jackson.

be sin, and through the commandment might become sinful beyond measure. ■ For we know that
the law is spiritual; but I am of the flesh, sold into
slavery under sin. " I do not understand my own
actions. For I do not do what I want, but I do the very
thing I hate. " Now if I do what I do not want, I agree
that the law is good. " But in fact it is no longer I that
do it, but sin that dwells within me. " For I know that
nothing good dwells within me, that is, in my flesh.
I can will what is right, but I cannot do it. " For I do
not do the good I want, but the evil I do not want
is what I do. " Now if I do what I do not want, it is
no longer I that do it, but sin that dwells within me.
■ So I find it to be a law that when I want to do what
is good, evil lies close at hand. " For I delight in the
law of God in my inmost self, " but I see in my members another law at war with the law of my mind,
making me captive to the law of sin that dwells in
my members. " Wretched man that I am! Who will
rescue me from this body of death? " Thanks be to
God through Jesus Christ our Lord! ■ So then, with
my mind I am a slave to the law of God, but with my
flesh I am a slave to the law of sin.

WHO·WILL
...
IN LOVE
OF CHRIST?

nor rulers

nor angel

nor things present

nor things to come

neither death nor life

nor anything

in all creation

8

THERE is therefore now no condemnation
for those who are in Christ Jesus. " For the
law of the Spirit of life in Christ Jesus has
set you free from the law of sin and of death. " For
God has done what the law, weakened by the flesh,
could not do: by sending his own Son in the likeness
of sinful flesh, and to deal with sin, he condemned
sin in the flesh, " so that the just requirement of the
law might be fulfilled in us, who walk not according to the flesh but according to the Spirit. " For those
who live according to the flesh set their minds on
the things of the flesh, but those who live according
to the Spirit set their minds on the things of the Spirit. " To set the mind on the flesh is death, but to set
the mind on the Spirit is life and peace. " For this reason the mind that is set on the flesh is hostile to God;
it does not submit to God's law—indeed it cannot;
" and those who are in the flesh cannot please God.
■ But you are not in the flesh; you are in the Spirit,
since the Spirit of God dwells in you. Anyone who
does not have the Spirit of Christ does not belong
to him. " But if Christ is in you, though the body is
dead because of sin, the Spirit is life because of righteousness. " If the Spirit of him who raised Jesus from
the dead dwells in you, he who raised Christ from
the dead will give life to your mortal bodies also
through his Spirit that dwells in you. ■ So then,
brothers and sisters, we are debtors, not to the flesh,
to live according to the flesh—" for if you live according to the flesh, you will die; but if by the Spirit you
put to death the deeds of the body, you will live. " For
all who are led by the Spirit of God are children of
God. " For you did not receive a spirit of slavery to
fall back into fear; but you have received a spirit of
adoption. When we cry, "Abba! Father!" " it is that
very Spirit bearing witness with our spirit that we
are children of God, " and if children, then heirs, heirs
of God & joint heirs with Christ—if, in fact, we suffer
with him so that we may also be glorified with him.
■ I consider that the sufferings of this present time
are not worth comparing with the glory about to
be revealed to us. " For the creation waits with ea-
ger longing for the revealing of the children of God;
" for the creation was subjected to futility, not of
its own will but by the will of the one who subjected it, in hope " that the creation itself will be set free
from its bondage to decay and will obtain the freedom of the glory of the children of God. " We know
that the whole creation has been groaning in labor
pains until now; " and not only the creation, but we
ourselves, who have the first fruits of the Spirit, groan
inwardly while we wait for adoption, the redemption of our bodies. " For in hope we were saved.
Now hope that is seen is not hope. For who hopes

Figure 13: *Fulfillment of Creation*, Thomas Ingmire.

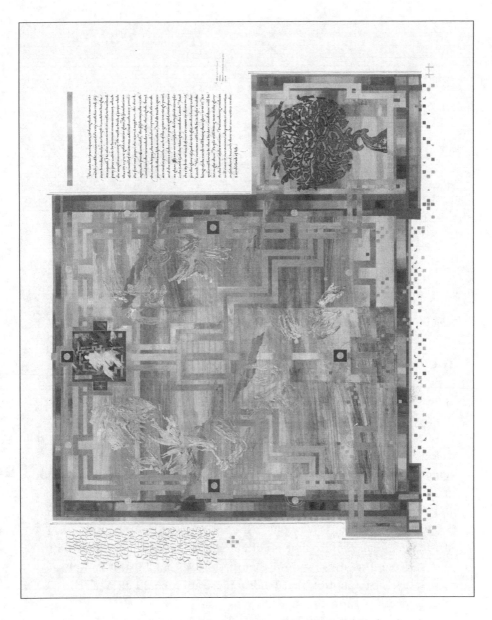

Figure 14: *Vision of the New Jerusalem*, Donald Jackson.

6

From a Mere Glance

Purposeful Reticence in Victorian Gospel
Illustration and *The Saint John's Bible*

SUE SORENSEN

THE ILLUMINATIONS OF *THE Saint John's Bible*, with their frequent emphasis
on the "tension between order and disorder, structure and chaos,"[1] may
appear to be unlikely conversation partners with Victorian religious art,
ostensibly so earnest and unadventurous. But while illustrated Bibles by
Jacques Tissot and Harold Copping, as well as the famous portrait of Christ
called *The Light of the World* by William Holman Hunt, might seem sentimental in twenty-first-century terms, these three influential Christian
painters (all born in the nineteenth century) were striving for freshness
and authenticity, their images of Jesus often surprisingly decentered and
beneficially mysterious. We would expect many of the postmodern images
of *The Saint John's Bible* to invite multiple stages of contemplation and complex movements of eye and mind, but these Victorian illustrators were also
edging toward the notion that biblical illustration could allow itself to be
both inspirational and enigmatic.

In my home city of Winnipeg, and probably in the churches in your
home communities, there are a number of stained glass windows reproduc-
ing *The Light of the World*, Hunt's Pre-Raphaelite painting of Christ standing in an overgrown orchard and knocking at a door.[2] For a time, *The Light*

1. Sink, *The Art of* The Saint John's Bible, 17.

2. See the website of St. Paul's Cathedral for an excellent reproduction. There are

of the World may have been the "most popular representation of Christ in the English-speaking world"[3]; it has even been called "a Protestant icon."[4] The image has now, to some extent, fallen from favour—I recently read a disapproving assessment of it as "a very British Christ, a very Victorian Christ . . . well-bred, restrained, and mild"[5]—but Hunt's painting continues to exert a certain power over me. It has had an influence on my aesthetic and spiritual life I'm not certain I can fully articulate, but I do know that one look at a reproduction in a book or on a postcard continues to provide me with reassurance, deep aesthetic pleasure, and, simultaneously, an urgent sense of call. Hunt supplies nothing like the explicit tension between structure and chaos explored in many of *The Saint John's Bible* illuminations, but nevertheless his painting communicates more than a hint of anxiety in its significant interplay of light and dark.

Hunt causes light to occur, rather wonderfully, at slightly impossible points throughout the canvas. The modest lantern at our bottom right manages to illumine (in ascending order, from the lowest part of the image) a grape vine and some fallen apples, the mark of the nail on Christ's left hand which holds the lantern, the folds of Christ's white robe, the wooden panel of the door and the upraised right hand which knocks, and, somewhat indistinctly, Christ's face. The only possible sources of illumination are the lantern, Christ's halo, and the stars in the night sky, but the halo and stars are much dimmer than the lantern. Looking carefully at the painting today I can see symbolic reasons for Hunt to draw our attention to the fallen apples and the vine—respectively, our human sin and our redemption. The same associative thinking helps with the spotlight on the mid-section of the door and on Christ's wounded lower hand, plotted at approximately the same latitude of the canvas: the door is my hard heart and the wounded hand indicates the sublime action which won my salvation. It's when my eye reaches the upper hand, caught in the act of knocking—although Christ faces not the door, but the viewer, with a countenance of intense sorrow and gentleness—that I ask how these multiple points of light could be functioning in this manner. Working on this essay is the first time I have been specifically aware of the multitude

two other versions with subtle differences—in Manchester Art Gallery and at Keble College, Oxford—but I will concentrate on the St. Paul's painting.

3. Avery-Quash, "The Light of the World," 34.

4. Bronkhurst, "The Light of the World," 119.

5. MacGregor, "The Abiding Presence," 193.

of symbolic objects and the first time I have wondered quite how the light in the painting works. The experience heretofore has been amazingly thoughtless on my part. But the message—of miraculous generosity, of supreme patience and kindness—reached me anyway. The viewer does not need to be explicitly alert to the symbolic features of Hunt's painting to benefit from the message of beneficence and compassion.

The painting occasioned, or solidified, a conversion experience for the artist himself,[6] and his intense engagement with the subject, which began with the first canvas in 1853, did not end until the third version was finished 50 years later. By this time Hunt had lost most of his eyesight and needed assistance to complete it. Although critics were dubious about the painting at its first appearance in the 1850s, with the public *The Light of the World* enjoyed enormous popularity, and this acclaim must have been a factor in the creation of the three versions—the last one, from St. Paul's Cathedral, went on tour, like an opera singer or a rock band. In Canada, South Africa, Australia, and New Zealand, people queued for hours to see it between 1905 and 1907, and one man reported a "vast crowd . . . gazing in silent wonderment, and many in adoration."[7] In addition to countless stained-glass adaptations, many (bad) poems had their origins in the painting, and Sir Arthur Sullivan composed an oratorio based on it in 1873.[8]

Although the painters of the Pre-Raphaelite Brotherhood later became associated with a style which was deeply sensuous, even embarrassingly exotic, at their beginning in the 1840s, they "strove for simplicity and sincerity" and hoped "to render nature . . . faithfully," in Ernst Gombrich's words.[9] (In this they followed, at least to some extent, the German Nazarene school of the early nineteenth century.) One of the matters Hunt was addressing in his landmark painting was how to handle Christian symbolism within the original Pre-Raphaelite commitment to natural setting and realism. For example, Hunt worried about how to present the face of Christ and therefore used multiple models. One of those, with beautiful strangeness, was the poet Christina Rossetti. This compound and feminine aspect may be one reason why this painting is beloved. Similarly, Christ's posture is humble and natural. Never again did Hunt manage this so well. The Christs in his

6. Bowness, *The Pre-Raphaelites*, 15.

7. Quoted in Avery-Quash, "The Light of the World," 34.

8. Excerpts of the poems can be found within George Landow's book about Hunt, *Replete with Meaning*, accessible on *Victorian Web*.

9. Gombrich, *The Story of Art*, 386.

other paintings often look contorted; as examples, see *The Shadow of Death* and *The Finding of the Saviour in the Temple*. But more than anything else, even through the questionable stained-glass reproductions I have seen, I am moved by the light which Christ both holds and is.

This light—soft, dim, beautiful—is in keeping with the pre-dawn gloom of the environment. The painting's temporal setting is that thorny but potentially rewarding twilight when all that is humanly wrong can be overwhelming and yet we are acutely susceptible to the possibilities of grace. And although Revelation's "Behold, I stand at the door and knock" is the prime scriptural mover of this painting, my response simultaneously involves that other Gospel knocking that Christians are invited to do in Matthew 7:7, "Ask, and it will be given you; search, and you will find; knock, and the door will be opened for you."[10] Many years ago, this painting and these scriptures became intertwined for me with two Metaphysical poems: John Donne's "Batter My Heart, Three-Personed God" (which involves the Savior knocking, strenuously) and George Herbert's "Love III," in which the speaker knocks, hesitantly, and the Savior welcomes: "But quick-eyed Love, observing me grow slack / From my first entrance in, / Drew nearer to me, sweetly questioning, / If I lacked any thing."

Hunt's painting has prompted for me an intuitive openness to a variety of ways of experiencing a welcoming Christ who stands at the doorway of salvation. Pausing now to use my reason, I see that the painting—and the way it has interacted with other scriptural and poetic depictions of knocking—has appealed to me not because of any explicit moral lesson on offer, but instead because of its invitational intimacy. The interplay of light and dark in the painting gratifies my love of enigma and ambiguity; the pre-dawn atmosphere supplies beautiful hints and possibilities rather than hard certainties. There has been a good thoughtlessness in the way I've received its evocative message of grace.

In the sixteenth century, the Jesuit writer Diego Jiménez, offering advice about using images in sacred meditation, said this: "Expect no spiritual growth (which Christ effects abundantly in souls open to Him in contemplation of His sacred life) from a mere glance at the pictures or wonder at their artistic beauty. Spend a whole day, even several days, with each image."[11] I acknowledge the good sense of that advice, but I wonder if the opposite might also pertain. Has Hunt's painting worked on me slowly, as

10. For a parallel passage, see Luke 11:9.
11. Quoted in Clifton, *Scripture for the Eyes*, 11.

Jiménez so wisely counseled, or has its message for me been revealed at a "mere glance"? The insights and influence happen, of course, in both ways (and more), but I am inclined toward the notion of the glance. My appreciation of *The Light of the World* has been momentary and spontaneous, based on dim possibilities and only partly comprehended ideas. Above all, my experience has been relational. Although I know that the painting (or the stained-glass window) is not Christ and could not really look like Christ, I have responded in a personal and rather unconscious way to a summons which, for many years, I did not even try to articulate.

In this notion of intuitive visual knowledge I am influenced by my reading of critic Robert Alter, who, in *The Art of Biblical Narrative*, is respectful of narrative "reticence," of words that are "selectively silent in a purposeful way."[12] Book designer Peter Mendelsund, in *What We See When We Read*, says something similar: "Maybe elaborate descriptions, like colorful descriptions, are misdirection. They seem to tell us something specific and meaningful (about a character, a setting, the world itself), but perhaps such description delights in inverse proportion to what it reveals."[13] In Alter's writings about, especially, the Hebrew scriptures, he encourages attention to "a sense of the unknowable and the unforeseeable," to "a sense of character as a center of surprise." Even though—or perhaps because—certain Biblical stories are, as Alter says, "laconic," characters like Rebekah, Jacob, and Joseph have nevertheless become "etched as indelibly vivid individuals in the imagination of a hundred generations." Alter promotes an awareness of Biblical narrators who display a "drastic selectivity."[14] This "drastic selectivity"—or reticence—is certainly not the same as comprehending by a "mere glance," but for my purposes here I am going to assume these concepts are near enough for us to be going forward with. The laconic and enigmatic representation of character, the momentary and intuitive visual experience can be surprisingly rich in impact.

The illuminations in *The Saint John's Bible*, most of them by Donald Jackson, are particularly effective at communicating rich and vivid meaning by means of a "mere glance." Although some of the paintings are traditionally representative, mimicking icons or offering tribute to artists of the late Middle Ages such as Giotto, many hover in the beautifully suggestive and vigorous precincts of abstraction and communicate their meanings, I would

12. Alter, *The Art of Biblical Narrative*, 115.
13. Mendelsund, *What We See*, 154.
14. Alter, *The Art of Biblical Narrative*, 126–27.

argue, intuitively. The stunning illuminations in Luke 23 and 24 offer Christ as a shimmering, golden almost-mirage, a gorgeous, blinding glow of wonder and power (see Figure 9, *Crucifixion*). One might be tempted to think of these suggestive shimmerings in *The Saint John's Bible* as something quite new—open, inclusive, and flexible—but there are elements of this evocative openness not only in Hunt's famous *The Light of the World* but also in beloved illustrated Bibles of the Victorian and Edwardian era.

It is difficult now to grasp with accuracy the intense affection many thousands of people had in the nineteenth and early twentieth centuries for certain illustrated Bibles. I am reflecting on the Copping Bible and the Tissot Bible, but one could also consider the 1865 Gustave Doré Bible. Although similar in popularity, it is different enough in conception and style that I decided against including it in this discussion. Harold Copping's Bible (1910) was commissioned by the Religious Tract Society in England, while a similar project (not an actual Bible) was the 1903 publication of *The Life of our Saviour Jesus Christ* by the French artist Jacques (sometimes anglicized as James) Tissot. These illustrations were for a time enormously popular, but they also suffered a fairly spectacular fall from fame. The Doré paintings are the most pointed example; after being viewed by millions in exhibition, they were stored and literally forgotten for several decades.[15] Despite the apparent widespread dissemination of the Copping Bible, while researching this paper I had difficulty locating one to examine, and my university librarian could find none in a Canadian library for me to borrow.

After being a painter of fashionable London and Paris, Tissot experienced a religious conversion in the 1880s and began a painstaking series of 365 New Testament paintings. Like the early Pre-Raphaelites, Tissot, at this stage in his life, had an essential commitment to realism. Therefore, he believed his new work warranted conscientious research and extensive travel in Palestine. In the late 1890s, when the paintings were exhibited, they were a sensation, with viewers who "sank to their knees, and literally crawled round the rooms in reverent adoration, sobbing and crying."[16] The paintings toured America and raised over $100,000 in admission fees— perhaps two or three million dollars today. For the book publication, Tissot received one million francs, and it was a considerable stylistic influence on D. W. Griffith's film *Intolerance*. Harold Copping is less known today,

15. Zafran, *Fantasy and Faith*, 157–70.

16. Wood, *Tissot*, 149, 155.

but references indicate that his Biblical illustrations were once celebrated.[17] The Copping Bible was a best seller, and the popularity of this Bible led to the London Missionary Society commission of *The Hope of the World* in 1915, which has been called the "most popular picture of Jesus produced in Britain in the twentieth century," an iconic image in British Sunday Schools just a few decades ago.[18]

Tissot and Copping had a parallel aesthetic, even spiritual practice, in their Biblical paintings, and in part this commitment to verisimilitude (as they might have termed it) is what penetrated to the hearts of their millions of viewers. Their method of illustration was a profoundly felt response to the Higher Criticism, that intellectual movement that created such anxiety amongst nineteenth-century Christians. Responding to their era's uneasy need to probe the historical accuracy of the Bible, Copping and Tissot, like Hunt, spent long periods of time in the Holy Land. They were determined to paint the light, landscapes, clothing, animals, and peoples of the Bible accurately—or as close to such accuracy as earnest northern Europeans could manage. This style now looks precise rather than accurate and is probably, to our eyes, sentimental. Yet sentiment is exactly what they were trying to avoid.[19] Careful and reverent, only occasionally do these paintings achieve vitality in modern or postmodern terms, but we should not lose sight of how meaningful these paintings were to a great many Victorians and Edwardians.

Opening a Copping Bible now (if you can lay your hands on one), the watercolors might seem fusty and antiquated; at his worst, Copping does indulge in Victorian quirks and exoticism.[20] His Christ is, strangely, a redhead, and his compositions can be histrionic. But *The Sower* and *The Prodigal Son* have intriguing lines of directional force that take us away from foursquare representation; there is a freshness to his landscapes of the Sea of Galilee that nudges us out of northern European or North American stereotypes of what the Holy Land is supposed to look like. His *Walk to Emmaus* is a good example of the kind of quiet revelation which Copping, at his best, could offer. It may be hard to capture the experience now—the Bible I viewed is a century old, the ink faded—but once the airy and natu-

17. Brewer, "Protestant Pedagogy," 267.

18. Brewer, "From Darkest England," 98.

19. Wood, *Tissot*, 155.

20. Although there is no easily accessible edition of Copping's paintings, individual works can be found via an online search.

ral colours of Copping's scene would, I suspect, have been novel, as would the lack of a halo or any complex symbolic treatment for Jesus. There is a humility to this painting, and also an appropriate sadness or downheartedness in all three figures that is counterintuitively refreshing. More than anything else—and here is where I refer you again to Robert Alter's concept of "the unknowable and the unforeseeable," of a "sense of character as a center of surprise"—Christ's eyes are vaguely painted, his face mysterious and hidden not only from his fellow walkers but also from us.

This painting attempts to draw you into this particular moment of grief; it is pre-revelation. We may suspect something remarkable is happening or about to happen, but we are compelled to stay within unknowing. Given the nineteenth century's well-known enthusiasm for certainty, sincerity, and optimism, Copping's painting is surprisingly ambiguous. There is no particular message or lesson on view. Instead we see mere companionship, if companionship can ever be mere. Christ is more upright than his fellow walkers, and his hand on a shoulder certainly indicates the support he offers the others. But the sadness of Christ's expression implies he is also in need of friendship. The relational qualities of this painting seem to me unlike typical Christian paintings of previous eras. The close proximity of the three walkers to each other underscores their mutual need. What is emphasized is Christ's vulnerability and humanity, his physical presence very close indeed to those with whom he walks.

Jacques Tissot had a far more involved career with Biblical illustration, which followed after his very worldly achievements as a painter of high society. In addition to the paintings within *The Life of our Saviour Jesus Christ*, Tissot also experimented with updating scriptural stories, and he had some success with paintings which moved the parable of the Prodigal Son into modern life. If you know Tissot's attractively "profane" oil paintings like *The Woman of Fashion* or *The Shop Girl*, you may find his Bible paintings unremarkable—after the vibrancy of his handsome young Victorian women, gorgeously and glossily arrayed, it can be hard to adjust to a certain flatness in the "sacred" watercolors. Tissot, like Copping, also paints Jesus as an apparent redhead, which can be puzzling. But there are several Tissot Biblical paintings which bear up particularly well.[21] As with Copping's *The Road to Emmaus*, the viewer may have a sensation of not knowing what is going to happen next when looking at Tissot's *Jesus Bear-*

21. The Brooklyn Museum has an extensive Tissot collection and makes the images available on its website.

ing the Cross. Christ's suffering is presented with relative restraint. There are many other individuals in the painting who vie for our attention; Jesus is not centrally positioned. The viewer of the painting is compelled to stay in the moment, "merely" to be present to Christ's humanity, sacrifice, and beauty. To wait and see.

Tissot did some subtle and surprising things with his compositions. The arrangement of his *Last Supper* is highly unusual. Christ and the disciples stand around a table, many of the figures having their backs to us; it can take a moment to decide which of the identically attired men is the Lord. The colors are muted, autumnal. The atmosphere speaks of a brotherhood (not, unfortunately, a sisterhood, but this was a century ago) and to a gathering of radical equality and humility. Compared to Tissot's version, Da Vinci's *Last Supper* looks self-consciously theatrical and artificial. For *The Death of Jesus,* Tissot places in the center of the picture not the cross, which is slightly to the left, but no less than five grieving women at Christ's feet. The intense darkness of a long, swirling black robe that one of them wears is the dominant emotional note, doubled and sustained by the ominously boiling gray sky. Perhaps most unusual about the arrangement of this Crucifixion is the way Tissot encourages the observer to enter the scene. There is a large, sombre space deliberately left for us in the midst of the female mourners. The space is at the heart of the composition and its message unmistakable: this is not something that happened long ago, but involves the viewer at this moment.

Not all of Tissot's paintings are so carefully considered; there are maudlin and melodramatic renderings. But if he had painted only his *Miracle of the Loaves and Fishes,* Tissot's Biblical project would be worth remembering. More than other representations I have encountered, Tissot's version of this miracle provides a sense of its material immensity. The first impression is one of abundance. People are everywhere; chaos could easily have won the day. But an unusual order has overtaken the potential chaos. The thousands of people being fed by Christ have been seated in zigzagging diagonal rows up the hill. These diagonals provide movement and complexity satisfying to the hungering eye. We probably do not know where to look first, and that is a marvelous thing. The viewer can experience, tangibly, how very many people were there, how very many were fed. In this composition, you have to do some work to find Jesus, and that is as it should be. *There* he is, you realize after a moment. He is a small but noble figure at upper right, working at a makeshift altar.

Many religious paintings allow us to locate Jesus too easily: precisely in the center, obvious in his divinity. Van Dyke, El Greco, Gauguin, Dali, even the non-Christian Chagall—we can think of dozens of artistic renderings of Christ which sacrifice mystery for certainty, even inevitability. These famous portrayals have great beauty and worth, yet may do little to involve us, to urge us to a rewarding search for Christ, to bring his experience close to our own. Tissot does not offer anything extraordinarily new with his less obvious Jesus; as Walter Melion has pointed out, in Dutch sixteenth-century Biblical prints Jesus could be compositionally "marginalized" and the viewer "presented with the problem of finding him, as a surrogate for the experience of spiritual discernment that parables elicit and dramatize."[22] Still, the dominant tradition paints Christ squarely in our sightlines. A reticent Jesus like the one in Tissot's *The Miracle of the Loaves and Fishes* is a Jesus we need to seek out and encounter. We need to climb up that crowded hill to achieve a closer acquaintance with that faraway, hard-working man, serving the basic needs of so many people. In *The Saint John's Bible*, a similar search for Jesus happens in *The Call of the Disciples*,[23] a wonderfully hectic image that draws the eye instructively through a multitude of our fellow Christians before we find the Savior himself. This search for Jesus may seem to counter my remarks about apprehending him "at a mere glance," but this search is not so much the act of contemplation or meditation but instead involves personal encounter. The point is meeting him, even stumbling across him: we are invited into the paintings for exploration.

Undoubtedly the Victorian and Edwardian depictions of Christ by Tissot, Copping, and Hunt are distinct from the illuminations by Donald Jackson and others in The Saint John's Bible, but they do begin to lay the groundwork for views of a modern or postmodern Christ more mysterious and more recognizably human than touchstone representations to which we have become accustomed in prominent art galleries and cathedrals. Among the most moving of Jackson's depictions of Christ is *The Word Made Flesh*, the frontispiece for the Gospel of John. The gold leaf used for Christ's body is, of course, opulent and stupendous, but other features in this illumination are more unexpected. The shape of the entire illustration is defiantly not square or rectilinear but seems to be inventing its own complex and intuitive geometry. The rich, dark, chaotic background of the cosmos actually shows its colors through the body of Christ, who both incorporates the

22. Melion, "Scripture for the Eyes," 23, 26.
23. John 1:35–51.

known universe and supersedes it. The golden figure is, to my eyes, indifferently gendered, which is bracing. Also refreshing is that the figure seems to stride toward us, not passively await us (as with far too many portrayals of Christ). Both the whirling cosmic background and the golden Christ are overwritten with delicate cursive lettering from Colossians 1, the words of a future epistle defying conventional concepts of time in their appearance here. Earthly logic dictates that John 1 should precede Colossians 1, but human time is undone and rewritten in an elegant palimpsest. This invigorating temporal upset is highlighted even more when we look closely and read in one of the verses of Colossians 1 that "He himself is before all things." Similarly, buttressing the verse "All things have been created through him and for him" is the technique: Jackson's lovely cursive lettering is written both on Christ and through Christ.

Jackson's *Resurrection* in John 20 offers us a regal but indeterminate figure, off-center and not facing us, who feeds our need of enigma, our hunger for the hooded, the ambiguous, even the nebulous (see Figure 11, *Resurrection*). The visual focus of the work is Mary Magdalene, in brilliant red, privileged to look into Christ's face while we must contemplate his glory reflected in her own. As Susan Sink points out, "Instead of seeing Jesus, we see him in her response."[24] The illumination emphasizes the tremendous contribution of Mary and her faith: Christ is regal, but so is Mary—his friend and our representative. The glance between Mary and Jesus indicates deep love; there is a certain bond between them which offers the hope that Christ can similarly befriend us. The intimacy of her outstretched hand says everything about the profound comfort Mary associates with Christ—and the rich colors of this painting strongly suggest her need will be answered. Even the framing of this image offers us divinity which beautifully bends and shifts. There is a decorative border, but it is variable and broken with brilliant slashes of color.

This Christ with his back to us connects to Copping's hooded, melancholy Christ of *The Road to Emmaus* and to Tissot's several off-center, stooped, even hidden Christs. In the same way, *The Transfiguration* in Mark 9 of *The Saint John's Bible* offers us a Christ whose face is, in Susan Sink's words, "both present and absent" (see Figure 6, *The Transfiguration*).[25] The experience is arresting and disturbing, both completely holy and very familiar.

24. Sink, *The Art of* The Saint John's Bible, 97.
25. Ibid., 72.

One of the most powerful paintings in *The Saint John's Bible* is the tour-de-force in the midst of Luke 15, illuminated by Donald Jackson with Aidan Hart and Sally Mae Joseph, usually called the *Luke Anthology* (see Figure 8, *Luke Anthology*). This painting illustrates not only the parable of the Good Samaritan but also the Prodigal Son, Lost Sheep, Lost Coin, and Dives and Lazarus. On the right side of the image, we have, from a preceding chapter, Christ with Mary and Martha. The calligraphy tells us "There is need of only one thing."[26] The marvels of the *Luke Anthology* are many: the amazing exuberance and energy, the healing vitality and unpredictability of the colors, and the way in which the simultaneity of the parables and the disrupted scriptural order defy any sense we might have that the Christian story should be simple or straightforward. The calligraphy in the middle panel must be read downwards from right to left—beautifully but appropriately disconcerting for many of us. The shape of the calligraphy has urgency; it leans into meaning like a person running. The rich tones of red and gold communicate blood and holiness: pain and redemption side by side. For me, the primary gift of this painting is its diagonal movement. The hesitant Christian may not be confident about approaching Christ's presence head-on, but this work invites us, if we wish, to approach obliquely, crookedly. At a glance, the *Luke Anthology* says that there are all sorts of ways to come to Christ or let Christ come to us.

It might seem perverse that this essay claims to be about the concept of reticence in Biblical painting, and yet I end on the energetic, bustling work which is the *Luke Anthology*. But to be reticent can mean to be beautifully wary, cagey, even evasive. From a "mere glance" we cannot tell everything about this illumination—we do need to spend "a whole day, even several days" discovering the complexity of its composition and the complexity of Christ's graciousness. As Michael Patella of *The Saint John's Bible* Committee on Illumination and Text has said, "The illuminations are not illustrations. They are spiritual meditations on a text."[27] Yet from a mere glance we can know this: a crooked, oblique, diagonal encounter is a valid encounter with the Gospel. This encounter may be unsettling and ambiguous, full of dim hints and partially-articulated insights. Yet these very qualities indicate how open and how radical Christ's welcome can be.

When I first encountered Donald's Jackson's *The Word Made Flesh* in *The Saint John's Bible*, I think I both did and did not notice an intriguing

---

26. Luke 10:42.

27. Quoted in Calderhead, *Illuminating the Word*, 112.

detail: a keyhole, hovering, at the left of the image. This rather homely object stands out in a somewhat incongruous manner, but it is utterly appropriate as a symbol for Christ as the means, the key, to salvation. Similarly, for years I did not see that the door at which Christ knocks in William Holman Hunt's *The Light of the World* has no external handle. The door must be opened from the inside, from our side. This can be hard to establish via a reproduction, but the statement "Crucial to the painting is that the door has no handle" is made in a booklet issued by St. Paul's Cathedral, *The Light of the World Decoded*. In other words, Christ will not demand entrance or force his way in: he seeks entrance. These are the sort of resonant symbolic details in a painting which may become apparent after a period of study and contemplation, or may be overlooked even then. Or equally, such perceptions may enter the unconscious, intuitive mind. However this perception happens, my argument is that both *The Word Made Flesh* and *The Light of the World* instantaneously communicate invitation and illumination. What that invitation is and how it happens will be highly personal and individual, but often a mere glance at the unsettling beauty of an off-center Savior will be more than enough welcome.

Bibliography

Alter, Robert. *The Art of Biblical Narrative*. New York: Basic Books, 1981.

Avery-Quash, Susanna. "The Light of the World." In *The Image of Christ,* edited by Gabriele Finaldi, 193–95. London: National Gallery, 2000.

Bowness, Alan. "Introduction." In *The Pre-Raphaelites*, 11–26. London: Tate Gallery, 1984.

Brewer, Sandy. "From Darkest England to The Hope of the World: Protestant Pedagogy and the Visual Culture of the London Missionary Society." *Material Religion: The Journal of Objects, Art and Belief* 1.1 (2005) 98–124.

———. "Protestant Pedagogy and the Visual Culture of the London Missionary Society." In *Religion, Children's Literature, and Modernity in Western Europe, 1750–2000,* edited by Jan de Maeyer et al., 263–70. Leuven: Leuven University Press, 2005.

Bronkhurst, Judith. "The Light of the World" and "The Awakening Conscience." In *The Pre-Raphaelites*, 117–21. London: Tate Gallery, 1984.

———. *William Holman Hunt*. New Haven: Yale University Press, 2006.

Calderhead, Christopher. *Illuminating the Word: The Making of The Saint John's Bible*. Collegeville, MN: Liturgical, 2005.

Clifton, James, and Walter S. Melion. "Introduction." In *Scripture for the Eyes: Bible Illustration in Netherlandish Prints of the Sixteenth Century*, edited by James Clifton and Walter S. Melion, 10–13. New York: Museum of Biblical Art, 2009.

Gombrich, Ernst. *The Story of Art*. 11th ed. London: Phaidon, 1967.

Hunt, William Holman. *The Light of the World*. St. Paul's Cathedral. http://Stpauls.co.uk.

Landow, George P. *Replete with Meaning: William Holman Hunt and Typological Symbolism*. 1979. *The Victorian Web*. Last modified December 2001. http://www.victorianweb.org/painting/whh/replete/light.html.

The Light of the World Decoded: A Resource Book for Teachers and Students. London: St. Paul's Cathedral Schools & Families Department, n.d.

MacGregor, Neil. "The Abiding Presence." In *The Image of Christ*, edited by Gabriele Finaldi, 32–35. London: National Gallery, 2000.

Melion, Walter S. "Scripture for the Eyes: Bible Illustration in the Sixteenth Century Low Countries." In *Scripture for the Eyes: Bible Illustration in Netherlandish Prints of the Sixteenth Century*, edited by James Clifton and Walter S. Melion, 14–106. New York: Museum of Biblical Art, 2009.

Mendelsund, Peter. *What We See When We Read*. New York: Vintage, 2014.

The Holy Bible, Containing the Old and New Testaments, according to the Authorised Version. Illustrated by Harold Copping. London: Religious Tract Society, 1910.

Sink, Susan. *The Art of* The Saint John's Bible: *A Reader's Guide to Pentateuch, Psalms, Gospels and Acts*. Collegeville, MN: Order of Saint Benedict, 2007.

Tissot, James [Jacques]. *The Miracle of the Loaves and Fishes*, and other paintings. Brooklyn Museum. http://brooklynmuseum.org/opencollection/.

————. *The Life of Our Saviour Jesus Christ: 365 Compositions from the Four Gospels*. New York: Werner, 1903.

Wood, Christopher. *Tissot*. New York: Little, Brown, 1986.

Zafran, Eric. "'A Strange Genius': Appreciating Gustave Doré in America." In *Fantasy and Faith: The Art of Gustave Doré*, edited by Eric Zafran, 143–47. New Haven: Yale University Press, 2007.

7

Picturing Words

The Gospel as Imaged Word in
Thomas Ingmire's Illuminations

DANIEL TRAIN

MOST OF US, IT seems safe to say, will look for the extraordinary visual images in *The Saint John's Bible* before we do anything else. Perhaps especially for those familiar with the daunting chunks of plain, black print in our modern Bibles, that instinct to first flip through the pages of *The Saint John's Bible* while scanning quickly for pictures or other items of visual interest will no doubt also be familiar. For better or worse, our eyes will inevitably be initially drawn to the images rather than words—maybe especially so, when we presume to already know what the words say.

To be sure, in this regard we are likely not much different than those who encountered works of illuminated Scripture over 400 years ago—the last time a project of this magnitude was attempted. In today's context, however, it is also evident that the creators of *The Saint John's Bible* face unique challenges. Beyond the obvious difficulty of needing to justify the expense of such a project in the light of far more efficient and economical technologies, a subtler hurdle is our modern tendency to take the existence of the printed word for granted. Perhaps unlike our medieval counterparts, the ubiquity and homogeneity of words in print makes it so that we are hardly even conscious of words as printed figures when we encounter them. Moreover, our unlimited access to a vast trove of consistent and endlessly repeatable typefaces has undoubtedly diminished our capacity to appreciate both the challenges and the unique pleasures of handwritten lettering.

To make matters worse, Western assumptions about printed words can often be doubly dismissive: on the one hand, we tend to think of the shape of letters in ink as serving an entirely utilitarian purpose, so much so that we often ignore the visible dimension altogether—as if the letters are mere temporary stand-ins or typographical widgets which become invisible as soon as they have served their function.[1] Furthermore, on the rare occasion when we do consider the aesthetic dimensions of letters, our overriding concern tends to be about whether a certain font is fashionable or on-trend—as if the shapes of words were merely a matter of taste and personal preference. Either way, it seems fair to say, the actual letters we use to create words are rarely taken very seriously.

Not surprisingly, contemporary calligraphers have chafed at these tendencies and perhaps none more so than Thomas Ingmire. Since 1977, when he became the first non-UK citizen elected into the prestigious Society of Scribes and Illuminators, Ingmire has been earning a reputation as a pioneer and boundary-pusher in his field because of his willingness to challenge both the status quo of traditional calligraphy and our modern obliviousness to the beauty and expressive potential of the very lines and shapes that make up written language.[2] Bruce Nixon describes Ingmire as an artist who has always been "fascinated by the pictorial possibilities of language, the word(s) as image, the immersion of language in an exhilarating atmosphere of visual invention."[3] Against the somewhat limited view of

1. Manfredo Massironi notes a distinction between Western and Eastern conceptions about print, especially in regards to poetry: "In both Japanese and Chinese society, the meaning of written poetry cannot be completely expressed unless it is rendered in elegant calligraphy that is consonant with the significance of the poem. In the same way that a poetic text must be read with the right emphasis and scansion, a written text must be visually finished with skill and sensitivity. This is an aspect that is completely ignored by Western culture, in which the abstraction of the word is considered sufficient to transmit its content independently from the visual representation." Massironi, *Codici,* 10.

2. Bruce Nixon explains that "although Ingmire never abandoned traditional calligraphy, during the past three decades he has been more involved with stretching the boundaries of the medium. He begins with texts, most often poetic, but this work tends to be performative, placing its emphasis on written language as a visual and indeed a pictorial medium supported by the kindred acts of reading and looking at art. In some of his own projects since the mid-2000s . . . he has challenged bedrock ideas of calligraphic practice, undisguised virtuosity and preciousness among them, in works of striking informality, fragility, and warmth of feeling." Nixon, *Things that Dream,* 16.

3. See also Janet Wilson's "Where Word and Image Meet—Thomas Ingmire" and

calligraphy as merely "beautiful writing," Ingmire has insisted on the capacity of the written word itself—its lines, colors, movement, and especially the space it occupies—to quite literally *image* meaning and not simply be its passive conveyor. Again, Bruce Nixon:

> In the sheer abundance with which Ingmire composes, he, and every calligrapher working a similar terrain, reminds us that language may be the most miraculous of human inventions, that we proceed at much peril with the technological impulse that longs to bind it in the sheen of the uniform and the ordinary, measuring words by their utilitarian value alone. If we allow our language to slide into banality, will not our lives follow it there? [Ingmire's] work wants us to look again at something whose true character is no less extraordinary for its ceaseless daily use. Maybe more so.[4]

For Ingmire, then, the physical manifestations of words are not only just as full of potential for imagination and ingenuity as other forms of artmaking, they are inseparable from the ideas that give rise to them. It's not just that language and thought can never be understood apart from the other. For Ingmire, the *physical form* of language is also intrinsic to the ideas it conveys. One might even say that for Ingmire there are no wordmakers who are not also image-makers.

So it comes as no surprise that Ingmire's illuminations in *The Saint John's Bible* are distinctive as works which seek to draw our attention again to the extraordinary capacity of letters and language. Even within a larger work that challenges at every turn our modern distinctions in the West between words and images (through, for example, its inclusion of marginal decorations which seamlessly overlap into columns of text or special treatments of certain passages with stylized letters and decorated capitals), Ingmire's contributions are immediately recognizable as pictures made from words. Here, the shapes and lines of the letters themselves insistently remind us of the function of written words to image something into being.[5]

Michael Gullick's *Words of Risk: The Art of Thomas Ingmire*.

4. Nixon, "Review: The Calligraphy of Thomas Ingmire."

5. To be sure, Ingmire's contributions employ a wide range of graphics, colors, and lines beyond the shapes of the letters. Moreover, many of the illuminations by other artists not only form a backdrop for words, but the words are embedded inextricably in the structure of the image of itself. Even so, Ingmire's contributions to *The Saint John's Bible* display a noticeably greater reliance on letters for their composition and structure, suggesting that the agent of the illumination is not so much the figural or decorative elements as much as the letters themselves.

Given, then, Ingmire's almost compulsive fascination with the capacity of the "word as image," and the distinctiveness of his contributions to *The Saint John's Bible*, Ingmire's illuminations afford readers an opportunity to reflect more deeply about not just the biblical passages in question, but the whole of Christian Scriptures and the story of the Gospel at its center. More specifically, Ingmire's aesthetic assumptions about the capacity of written letters to convey the "miracle" of human language—this deep hope in the meaning-making potential of words as images—can both illuminate and be illuminated by the doctrinal and ecclesial assumptions which undergird the production of an extraordinary work like *The Saint John's Bible*. Here too, art and theology are mutually instructive.

On the one hand, Ingmire's work can not only revitalize our understanding of particular passages of Holy Scripture, but through its reconstruction of language in a self-consciously visual form, it draws our attention again to the theological utterance at the heart of all biblical interpretation.[6] Again and again, Ingmire's images bear witness to the Triune God who declares "I AM" throughout all space and time, and who has done so supremely in the life, death and resurrection of Jesus Christ. As the Word who "became flesh and made his dwelling among us" (John 1:14), the "image of the invisible God" (Col. 1:15), and the "exact imprint of God's very being" (Heb. 1:3), Christ is the word-image *par excellence* who reconciles all things (2 Cor. 5:18)—including the Old and the New Testaments—despite our penchant for self-deception and blind misinterpretations of God's Word. In other words, Ingmire's calligraphic illuminations reverberate with the Good News that the Triune God is in covenantal relationship with all Creation, a covenant enacted and sustained by God's Word.

On the other hand, the theological and hermeneutical principles motivating a work such as *The Saint John's Bible* can offer a corrective to a more modern aesthetic philosophy that assumes that visual presentations are held captive or reduced by our desire to discern meaning in them. Paradoxically, at times Ingmire himself embraces these principles and assumes that legibility and intelligibility are damaging restrictions upon a

---

6. In this context, Bruce Nixon's description of calligraphy's unique capacity seems especially promising for the work of theology and biblical interpretation: "If the calligrapher does indeed long to transform words into pictures, the tensions that flow from this need, which we feel in the very letters on the page, can return us to reading as a physical activity, a bodily experience of looking that, if we examine it closely, is ultimately inseparable from reading as an intellectual and imaginative activity." Nixon, *Things That Dream*, 22.

much higher good: individual creativity. Though Ingmire acknowledges the significance of the "connection between the visual image and the meaning of the words,"[7] he also sometimes describes their opposition as ultimately irreconcilable.[8] For example, in a handbook he prepared for training calligraphers, he concludes that "the success of calligraphy . . . lies in its ability to completely seduce the viewer—to cast a spell on the viewer by its forms—to gain the total attention of the viewer—to take the viewer away from the text."[9]

In making such comments (outside the context of *The Saint John's Bible* project), Ingmire no doubt is trying to challenge and revivify calligraphy as an art form that has become calcified and uncertain of its orientation amid technological innovations in digital printing. Nevertheless, as we will see, Ingmire's own work in *The Saint John's Bible* challenges the assumption that words achieve their fullness or independence when they escape meaning and intelligibility. But the choice is not simply between legibility and total abstraction, nor is the visual always locked into a zero-sum game with the verbal. Legibility, need not be, as Arne Wolf suggests, "the enemy of creativity."[10] Words or letters with recognizable referents need not be reductive—they can point to a reality that is both present and beyond. And this, I hope to show, is an absolutely crucial implication of the Gospel message at the heart of the very texts which inspire Ingmire's work: the Word "through whom all things were made" (Jn 1:3) and which makes "all things new" (Rev 21:5) is made a legible image in the life, death, and resurrection of Jesus Christ.

---

7. Ingmire, *Codici*, 48.

8. According to Ingmire, the "problem" modern calligraphy must address is that "the rules of visual language and the rules of verbal language stand almost in opposition to each other." Ibid., 54.

9. In the same text, Ingmire approvingly quotes Massironi's assessment of modern calligraphy: "The function of writing via typography once again gave calligraphy the freedom to inherit its ancient independence from the word. It was once again free to amuse itself at the expense of words." Ibid., 19

10. Ingmire quotes this in *Codici*, 19.

Picturing "I AM": The Word Made Image
in the Gospel of John

Just a few pages after the exquisite frontispiece to the Gospel of John,[11] readers encounter another superb illumination which similarly encapsulates the Gospel story at the heart of a Christian approach to the Scriptures: the Triune God's self-revelation and covenantal relationship with all of creation (see Figure 10, *I Am Sayings*). Unlike the John frontispiece however, Ingmire's *I Am Sayings*, relies almost exclusively on letters and abstract graphic elements to convey Jesus's repeated declarations of his divine Sonship. Quite literally, the words themselves become the image. And this, a feature that is characteristic of Ingmire's work more generally, certainly resonates with a major theme of John's Gospel. Moreover, it has crucial consequences for how we then approach not just the rest of the Christian Scriptures but the work of Christ's body, his church.

Ingmire's *I Am Sayings* references five distinct proclamations from Jesus about himself in the Gospel of John. "*I am* the Bread of Life" Jesus declares to a stunned audience in John 6:35. Later, just after he grants a mob the permission to stone a woman so long as they first prove themselves sinless, Jesus says to a similarly shocked audience, "*I am* the light of the world" (8:12). Likewise, after healing a blind man to the dismay of the Pharisees who protest, "Surely we are not blind, are we?" (9:40), Jesus tells them that "anyone who does not enter the sheepfold by the gate . . . is a thief and a bandit" (10:1). Anticipating their bewilderment and confusion, Jesus makes his meaning perfectly clear: "Very truly, I tell you, *I am* the gate for the sheep." Later, to the disciples who want more explicit directions about where to find Jesus when he leaves them, Jesus says, "*I am* the way, the truth, and the life" (14:6). And not long after, Jesus further declares, "*I am* the true vine, and my Father is the vine grower" (15:1).[12]

These five "I Am" statements correspond to the five vertical columns which provide the overarching architecture for Ingmire's image. For each column, the graphic elements are more densely layered at the bottom and

---

11. As others have shown (see David Jeffrey's essay in this volume), Donald Jackson's frontispiece is itself a kind of visual argument for the theological and scriptural foundations at the heart of *The Saint John's Bible* project.

12. Crucially, in the verses immediately following, John's audience begins to see that what all of these strange self-declarations amount to is an utterly radical account of what it means to abide with God. "Abide in me as I abide in you" says Jesus, for "*I am* the vine, and you are the branches" (15:1–7).

gradually recede into white spaces or shapes which are evocative of celestial luminaries. This has the effect of creating an impression of upward movement and suggests that picture is to be "read" from the bottom up.

It is perhaps significant, then, that the only column which reaches the top of the page without being interrupted by the white space and heavenly lights is the one corresponding to Christ as the Vine, a passage in which Jesus explicitly tells his disciples that they may abide in Jesus in the same way that Jesus abides in the life of God the Father (15:3–10). In a visual way, the illumination is subtly reiterating the full expression of the "I AM sayings" as a whole: Christ is not simply the *means* for "reaching" God; rather, any genuine encounter with God necessarily implies having a far richer, relational account of abiding with and dwelling in the Triune life. In other words, by saying "*I am*," Christ is proclaiming himself as both the *means* and *end*—the joy made complete (15:11).

Moreover, the structure of the image is clearly reminiscent of the frontispiece to the book of Genesis, which depicts the seven days of creation in similar vertical columns, a theme Ingmire explicitly echoes in his Romans 8 illumination (see Figure 1, *Creation* and Figure 13, *Fulfillment of Creation*). Much more could be said about how these visual echoes reverberate throughout *The Saint John's Bible* to instill a practice of reading a particular passage in conversation with the whole of Scripture. For now, it is perhaps enough to simply anticipate a point I will develop more fully: Ingmire's image, like John's Gospel, seeks to prompt a re-reading of the whole of Scripture in light of Jesus' radical claim to Divine Sonship as the Word made image, *through* whom and *for* whom all things were made (1 Col. 1:16).

To that end, in the *I Am Sayings* the colors and lines in each column are abstract and non-representational but nonetheless are suggestive of the central metaphors or word-pictures Christ employs. For example, the middle column's wave-like shapes in blue tones represent "the Way" and the last column on the right consists of a series of zig-zagging lines filled in shades of maroon, as if to suggest the vine and vineyard Jesus describes. More explicitly, in the first column, the many overlapping almond-shaped, elliptical spheres in shades of brown and gold bring to mind loaves of bread. Another name for this shape, the *vesica piscis* or "fish bladder," also draws out a further resonance with the popular Christian symbol of the *ichthys* or "Jesus fish." Interestingly, this symbol is itself inspired by an acrostic of Greek letters (ΙΧΘΥΣ) and functioned as a kind of shorthand or code in the early church to proclaim, "Jesus Christ, Son of God, Savior."

Indeed, in the second and fourth columns, Ingmire echoes this very practice of using letters to make pictures. Using white block letters against a teal-blue background, the words "THE GATE" form a striking depiction of an actual gate near the base of the column. The words then gradually dissolve into simple squares (suggestive of modern, low-resolution pixelation) as we move up through the column's successive layers of letters. In other words, the letters themselves not only name but *enact* a kind of barrier which gradually opens into—indeed, becomes a gateway for—an open space filled with light, where the boundaries between the columns have been blurred.

This breaking in of light is even more explicitly conveyed in the fourth column where the letters for "I AM THE LIGHT" appear in such a way as to suggest a window of shattered glass. Unlike the other columns, the jagged, overlapping boarders of the letters are disorderly and colored in black and white, except for a central portion where the barely legible letters "AM" are filled in gold. A few slivers or shards of gold filigree are scattered throughout the column, much like they are in the upper, "heavenly" register. But this sharp contrast from the colorful, carefully-proportioned lines in the other columns not only evokes a light which breaks in and illuminates everything else, but suggests that Christ's self-proclamations disrupt everything, shattering the conceptions of all of us who, perhaps like the Pharisees, say to ourselves in disbelief, "Surely, we are not blind, are we?"

Indeed, the extraordinary disruption of Jesus' radical claims about his relationship to God the Father, and thereby of his own Divinity, is made clear by the bottom-most section of the illumination. Using the same color palette as the columns above, the architectural "foundation" of the image is composed primarily of the four letters, "YHWH." As with the "I Am the Light" column, the letters are neither uniform nor precisely demarcated from their surroundings. The letters are not immediately intelligible, and readers will no doubt initially hesitate to proclaim with confidence what they see. Thus, the effect here is not simply to suggest a shattering or disruption in color and shape, but also to create a degree of uncertainty and ambiguity. Perhaps unlike our modern typographical conventions, wherein precision and consistency are paramount to achieving maximum legibility, the "meaning" that these letters point to is not precise or closed.

This too, it seems, is exactly the point. As many readers will know, these four letters (also known as the tetragrammaton) are a transliteration in Latin characters of the Hebrew four-letter word for God. Traditionally, out of reverence for the holiness of God's name, many Jewish communities refuse to pronounce these characters. Some Jewish communities even follow strict rules about how and where the name can be written, especially if the materials bearing the letters will be disposed of or can be erased easily.

Thus, the appearance of these letters in the context of the *I Am Sayings* is remarkable for several reasons—though "remarkable" seems not nearly a strong enough word. First, in keeping with the tradition of Christian Biblical interpretation, Ingmire's image makes explicit the link between Jesus' self-proclamations and the voice which speaks to Moses from the burning bush, naming Godself as "I Am that I Am." Like the rest of John's Gospel, the image thus makes the unmistakable (though no less radical) claim that Jesus is indeed One with the God of Abraham, Isaac, and Jacob.

However, as an image composed of letters (some of which are so holy they ought not to be uttered), Ingmire's illumination drives home the radical claims of the Gospel in a way that perhaps only an image can: the Word who was *with* and *is* God (whose spoken self-revelation as I AM is the basis of God's covenant with the Jewish people) is indeed made image in the very flesh of a Jewish man named Jesus Christ. Not only is Jesus proclaiming himself to be God, but the ineffable has been made visible; the God of unspeakable holiness has taken on human flesh and blood.[13] Ingmire's illumination points us back to the radical claims of the prologue: not simply that the Word (*logos*) was in the beginning, was with God, and indeed, *was* God (1:1), but most shockingly that "the Word became flesh and lived among us" (1:14). Moreover, Jesus is the Word-image about whom all the words of Christian Scripture speak.[14]

Thus, as the Gospel hearer's understanding of what it means for God to dwell with God's people is utterly transformed, the very letters we employ to refer to God are themselves transfigured. No longer are letters mere

13. Aidan Nichols explains it this way: "The Word incarnate renders the absent God present; in Christ the signifier *par excellence,* God the signified (equally *par excellence*) is perfectly expressed. Such a supremely successful act of the sensuous 'presencing' of an absence, an act duly represented in the language of the New Testament, furnishes the final validation of a logorythmic world where the patterns of language give access to nature in its actual order and course." Nichols, *Christendom Awake,* 60.

14. Nicholas Boyle explains that in the context of those who believe that "the Old Testament is Revelation only insofar as it is the announcement of an obligation whose fulfillment is unimaginable and whose origin is unnameable," the Gospel's good news is that "the requirement of the Law has been met, the unfulfillable obligation has been fulfilled, and the invisible and transcendent Law, and so its unnameable source, has been made visible in the death of a man born subject to it." Boyle, *Sacred and Secular Scriptures: A Catholic Approach to Literature,* 90.

signifiers for an utterly transcendent, abstract, invisible, unspeakable signified. In so far as they point not to more words but a person, our words participate (in their own, limited way) in God's self-revelation through Christ. In the light of Christ, letters as images need not simply remind us of absence and distance—of a reality which is lacking or missing. Like images, these too offer a re-presentation which is nonetheless a kind of presence, and thus can remind us of the God who is *present* among us.[15]

Equally significant, as the full reference of YHWH becomes clearer, our understanding of what it means for *us* to dwell with God is also transfigured. And doing so may involve, as the images of *The Saint John's Bible* attest, a re-reading of God's utterances elsewhere in Scripture in light of Jesus who is the bread, the light, the gate, the way, and the true vine.

Picturing "I AM": The Word Made Image in the Ten Commandments

Much like his illumination in the Gospel of John, Ingmire's *Ten Commandments*[16] is also composed of vertical columns (in this case, four) and prominently features another "I Am" saying (see Figure 4, *Ten Commandments*). Here too, the shapes, lines, and colors of the letters themselves function as essential, structural elements of the overall composition. And, as with my assessment of Ignmire's Gospel illumination, here too the inextricable interplay between word and image seems precisely the point.

Unlike the Gospel illumination, however, in *Ten Commandments* the graphic elements begin to dissolve in the *lower* register, suggesting (at least initially) that the image is to be "read" from the top down. The small, isolated letters floating (seemingly at random) at the bottom of the image pose a stark contrast to the bold, gold leaf, unpunctuated letters in the upper half of the page: "HERE I AM I AM THE GOD OF YOUR FATHER I AM THE

---

15. Natalie Carnes describes a kind of "iconoclasm" at the heart of how all images operate in so far as they present a "likeness" which is not identical to the referent in every respect: "As likeness appears in a stratum of unlikeness, so presence dawns in absence. In itself—in its own literal existence—the image is not this presence. . . . It confers a presence beyond itself. It mediates, that is, presence-in-absence. Absence, then, names the condition for the possibility of imaging. The image presents what it is not, and in the presentation of the 'is not,' the 'is'—the literal image—recedes." Carnes, *Image and Presence: A Christological Reflection on Iconoclasm and Iconophilia*, 6.

16. In Jewish tradition, these are referred to as the 10 Words.

LORD YOUR GOD." The choice and presentation of these words is striking for several reasons.

First, though Ingmire has rightly drawn attention to the often-ignored preface to the Ten Commandments in Exodus 20—"I am the Lord your God, who brought you out of the land of Egypt, out of the house of slavery"—Ingmire also includes references from elsewhere in the Scripture. Most notably, the phrase "I am the God of your Father" echoes YHWH's declaration to Moses from the burning bush in Exodus 3. The phrase is repeated elsewhere in the Christian Scriptures: for example, when God reminds Isaac of God's covenant with his father Abraham in Genesis 26:24 or in Acts 7:32, when Stephen testifies before the Sanhedrin just prior to his martyrdom. Similarly, the columns in the background explicitly put these words into a larger history. Susan Sink explains that the four columns represent four key points in Israel's history: the burning bush, the first Passover (suggested by red shapes intersecting at sharp angles), the Red Sea Crossing (with similarly angular shapes in blue and white), and the twelve pillars being erected at the base of Mount Sinai.[17] By adding the phrase here, Ingmire thus brilliantly situates the Commandments within 1) God's prior revelation of God's self, and 2) God's covenantal promises for God's people—in both the Old and New Testaments.

Secondly, Ingmire's placement of the letters not only alludes to other Scriptural references but itself becomes a way of interpreting this passage. Because there is no punctuation, the top line in Ingmire's image reads, "HERE I AM I AM." Again, this is a clear allusion to God's response to Moses' request in Exodus 3 to know the name of the one who sends him: "I AM [who/that] I AM." This seems to be further supported in the image by a third "I AM" a few lines below which is placed directly on top of the most recognizable graphic element on the page—a burning bush. Whereas in Ingmire's Gospel illumination "YHWH" quite literally serves as the architectural foundation for Jesus's "I Am" claims (despite not being immediately legible), in the Ten Commandments the first thing readers will see in clearly defined letters at the top of the page is God's declaration of God's name, though in this case there is no ambiguity and no hesitancy to pronounce the unpronounceable.

Finally, because the font remains consistent with the other words that God speaks, Ingmire seems to be crediting God with also saying the words, "Here I Am." This phrase does not appear in the context of Exodus 20,

17. Sink, *The Art of* The Saint John's Bible, 27.

and when it does appear elsewhere in Scripture, it is typically the words of the one *responding to* God's immediate address (as in Genesis 22:1, 31:11, 1 Samuel 3:4 or Isaiah 6:8). The phrase also occurs in Exodus 3:4, when God calls out Moses' name from the burning bush. Many English translations make it clear that Moses says these words in response to hearing his name, but others (including the NRSV-CE) use a more ambiguous "And *he* said, 'Here I am,'" which perhaps could be read in the English translation as referring to either God or Moses. Either way, Ignmire's image transforms the typical use of the phrase from the response of one who has been called by God, to an emphatic declaration of God's abiding presence as the introduction to the Ten Commandments. That is, as readers of this image, we cannot ignore that the first words we hear from God are "Here I am." And this unambiguous declaration of God's presence, prior to our reception of the conditions for a covenantal relationship with the very One who is the ground of all existence (the I AM who makes everything else "to be"), ought to radically influence how we receive the words that follow.

All this is further emphasized by the dramatic contrast between those opening, self-descriptive words in gold and the increasingly cluttered and chaotic enumeration of the commandments themselves. The closely spaced, black letters on (and sometimes behind) a busy background of lines and varying colors establish a clear divergence from the letters in the upper register. Susan Sink notes, "The familiar words of the commandments, stenciled in Stone Sans typeface as though engraved on tablets, eat through the colored background."[18] Just as clearly though, the words themselves seem to dissolve into the background, especially in the proclamation of the second commandment: "You shall not make for yourself an idol, whether in the form of anything that is in heaven above, or that is on the earth beneath you" (Ex 20:4). In fact, this is the last commandment that is completely legible; the others simply fade into an increasingly colorless jumble of shapes and shadows, where eventually just a few letters, much smaller in size, appear to float in complete isolation on the parchment.

This stark difference in legibility between upper and lower halves prompts the key interpretive questions posed by this image: what causes the dissolution of God's words? Why do the commandments seem to literally fall apart, especially in light of the commandment which prohibits making "idols" (or, as some translations say, "images") in the form of anything above or beneath? Is this a comment on the limits, if not outright failure, of human

18. Ibid., 27.

language to "image" God's word through letters? Might Ingmire's reluctance to render the other commandments legible be itself a way of taking to heart the second commandment's prohibition? In other words, what is the relationship between the dissolution of words and the larger image in which they play an essential part? Does the image, like the letters, announce its limited capacity to mean, or to convey God's message? Or does the illumination as a whole succeed where the individual letters fail?

And is this perhaps also simply a reminder about the astonishing rate at which the Israelites fail to live up to the terms of this covenant? Such an interpretation is encouraged by the rightmost column, which references the twelve pillars that were erected as symbols of the people's own promise in response to the commandments: "All the Lord has spoken, we will do and we will be obedient" (Ex 24:7).[19] These words appear near the base of the fourth column in gold letters, but in a much smaller font. And the fact that this response from the people seems to overlap the upper and lower halves is perhaps subtly suggestive of the people's ambivalence within the biblical text (and in Igmire's own image). For even though the people of Israel have already twice promised to "do" the word of the Lord, as soon as Moses ascends Mount Sinai to receive the two stone tablets upon which God writes words with his own finger (31:18, 32:16), the people of Israel give their wealth to Aaron and ask him to make them an idol—an image which has no real transcendent referent and whose signification is as hollow as the molds used to make it.

In the context of Ingmire's image, then, the words of the Israelites' promise sound both righteous and utterly foolish. As the Old Testament scriptures will attest, this promise to "do" and obey God's word rings hollow again and again, undermining the covenant God makes with God's people. In stark contrast to the scripture's repeated declaration of the God who is "I AM," the more God's people promise to be obedient, the less their words mean anything. Thus, for every reminder of God's faithfulness that this image evokes, it is also a reminder of our own limitation and hence the limitations of human language—words quite often mean

19. Interestingly, this is the second time this phrase occurs. The first time, the people respond to Moses's oral account of "*the words* of the Lord and all the ordinances," saying, "All the words that the Lord has spoken we will do" (24:3). The response Ingmire seems to be drawing on, however, occurs just a few verses later after Moses writes down the words of the Lord and reads to them from the "book of the covenant" (24:7). What the story clearly highlights in each case is that God's covenant is always an exchange of words.

much more (or much less) than we think they do, despite our sometimes idolatrous confidence in them.

Nevertheless, precisely because of this stark reminder about our human penchant for making false images, Ingmire's *Ten Commandments* illumination echoes the Gospel message animating not just his *I Am Sayings* illumination in the Gospel of John but *The Saint John's Bible* project as a whole. For if the top-down structure of Ingmire's *Ten Commandments* is suggestive of the gradual dissolution of God's direct word as humanity fails to heed it, then the bottom-up structure of the *I Am Sayings* in John is itself suggestive of the one through whom the conditions of the covenant are fulfilled and restored. As Jeffrey Bilbro says, "Jesus keeps these words when we have failed to do so, and in his life and person they are intelligible."[20] Taken together, the full implication of these two illuminations from the two Testaments becomes clear—the whole of Christian Sacred Scriptures is just that, a proclamation of the Word living among us. Because Jesus Christ as the Word made flesh is the "exact imprint of God's very being" (the KJV says the "express image of his person") and "sustains all things by his powerful word," the Christian Scriptures—whether through word, image, or both—resound with the good news of God's self-revealing, abiding, promise to all Creation: "Here I AM." For Ingmire (and for *The Saint John's Bible* more generally), this means that even the very lines we use to make words visible can participate in Christ's—and thereby the Church's—mission to *be* the "image of the invisible God."

Picturing Christ's Body:
The Words of Institution and Calligraphic Intelligibility

We could point to many other Thomas Ingmire illuminations in *The Saint John's Bible* to further exemplify his distinct way of making theologically-rich images out of mostly words and letters. In many, if not all of these, we can again identify the familiar emphasis on God's very words entering into the narrative and the content of these divine self-revelations as yet a further realization of God's covenantal relationship with God's creation.

For example, the three-image sequence in the book of Job creates an arresting visual dramatization of the dialogue between God and Job in Chapters 39–42. In the first image, the page itself appears to be assailed by the series of accusative questions God poses to Job; the letters and phrases

20. Private correspondence.

erupt every which way from a similarly chaotic background, disrupting the orderly columns of handwritten text. Readers will instantly perceive the barrage of questions as a kind of indignant intrusion—not just into Job's grief, but also into the larger story of Job's life and perhaps into our own wrestling with God and tragedy.

In the second image, there are similar fragments of phrases from God's direct speech to Job, though here again (as with the *Ten Commandments* illumination) the words, "I AM THE LORD YOUR GOD" appear gilded in gold at the top. Here too, the words are explicitly contrasted with Job's own chastened response in a different typeface and much smaller font: "I had heard of you by the hearing of the ear. But now my eye sees you" (42:5). Unsurprisingly, this vision comes in the context of God's speech which is itself replete with poetic images. And by juxtaposing God's proclamation with Job's response, Ingmire creates yet another subtle reminder of God's direct word itself becoming a kind of image which Job can finally see. Here too, as I have been suggesting, Ingmire's images create the opportunity for his own readers to have a similar experience of a hearing which turns into a seeing of God's Word.

In the final image, the upper register again features a chaotic barrage of words and letters, though this time these are not God's utterances but rather phrases gathered from much earlier in the book where the narrator recounts the many horrific events that befall Job and his household. Immediately beneath this, again in a typeface unique to Job's voice, is his response to God's speech: "I know that you can do all things, and that no purpose of yours can be thwarted." Most strikingly, undergirding the entirety of Job's final, faithful affirmation in the midst of descriptions of unthinkable tragedy which rain down like deadly arrows on his words, are the words from Revelation 21:4 "He will wipe every tear from their eyes, death will be no more, mourning and crying and pain will be no more for the first things have passed away." In sharp contrast, the thin-line letters appear against a kaleidoscope of shapes and colors which fill in all the spaces between, suggestive of mortar on a rainbow of brick. Indeed, it seems clear that these letters hold together and support the kind of eschatological hope Job proclaims and which Christian readers have drawn from in their interpretation of this difficult story throughout millennia.

Taken as a sequence, then, these images not only exemplify Ingmire's deep hope in the capacity of the shapes and lines of letters themselves to make meaning visible, but they also reiterate the intra-textual character of

The Saint John's Bible.[21] For the makers and interpreters of The Saint John's Bible, because the Christian Scriptures begin and end with the Word made flesh dwelling among us by the work of the Spirit, the whole of Scripture is made present in any one of its parts. God's speech—his very presence in words and the Word—resounds throughout all Scripture.

This abiding presence made manifest in both the Scriptures and the life of the Church is delightfully expressed in Ingmire's simple yet powerful rendering of two key passages in the book of 1 Corinthians. In the first, Ingmire takes the words of Institution for the Eucharist (1 Cor. 11:23–26) and creates an unbroken block of letters which are so close together that the eye has trouble making out the individual words. At the bottom of the image, the space in between the letters is filled in maroon tones and gradually recedes as the eye moves upward. Thus, the colors and shading of these letters suggest a Eucharistic cup, "the new covenant in my blood" (11:25) that Jesus proclaims during his final meal with his disciples. Using only letters and colors, Ingmire has skillfully helped his readers to quite literally see the cup which is both a remembrance and proclamation of Christ's sacrifice "until he comes" (11:26). The words of institution themselves re-present the image of the cup, itself an image of Christ's sacrifice.

I would also argue, however, that the full meaning of this image can only be understood in dialogue with a similar textual representation which appears on the opposing page. Here, Ingmire takes up the all-too familiar discourse on love from Chapter 13 but re-presents it so that it both illuminates and is illuminated by the words of Institution. Accordingly, Ingmire takes the first four verses of the chapter which focus on the failure and emptiness of Spiritual gifts without love and presents them in mostly black, white, and grey lettering in the upper-right hand of the page. The letters extend well beyond the margins of the text and are in angular lines pointing in various directions, creating a disruption on the page that is not unlike "the noisy gong" and "clanging cymbal" which herald the nothing-ness of work without love.

Moving down the page and to the left (against our Western patterns of reading), however, the image takes up the constructive, poetic descriptions of love which fill out the rest of the chapter: "Love is patient; love is kind; love is not envious or boastful." Here, in sharp contrast to the disorderly, black and white of the preceding verses the letters make a nearly uniform block of text in parallel lines that extends just slightly beyond the bottom margin. In a perfect inversion of the Eucharist passage, the spaces between the letters in

21. Patella, *Word and Image,* 13–15.

the uppermost portion of the block are filled in and gradually recede as the eye moves downward. This time, however, the spaces are colored in with the full spectrum of the rainbow, a pattern that gradually extends to the letters below and creates the impression of vertical columns of blended, overlapping colors. The typeface matches the piece on the opposite page, and the letters are also spaced in such close proximity that the words are not immediately legible. Rather, what impresses the reader first is the brightness of the colors and a pattern which Fr. Patella describes as a "diaphanous silk scarf."[22]

Indeed, together these two illuminations present a kind of tapestry that weaves together God's self-revelation and covenant with God's people, the love re-presented in the bread and the wine, and the demanding love which is required of those who participate in this remembrance. In distinct, yet clearly complementary ways these two illuminations create a word-picture for the viewers of the word made flesh in the Eucharist and in the life of those who obey Jesus' command "to love one another as I have loved you" (John 13:34). And this, we would do well to remember, is the statement that prompts his disciples to admit that they do not know what to do or where to go. Jesus' response, as Ingmire can help us to hear and see again, includes both a word-image and the image-word: "I AM the Way, the Truth, and the Life" (John 14:6).

Moreover, Ingmire's illuminations can help us see that God's act of creation through the Word made image does not end in Genesis but is rather the very grammar of God's ongoing relationship with the whole cosmos. The word that creates and recreates all things is the very same word that eternally proclaims in covenant with all of creation: "Here I AM." Indeed, this is the final vision offered to us in the book of Revelation: "See, the home of God is among mortals. He will dwell with them; they will be his peoples; and God himself will be with them. . . . See, I am making all things new" (21:3–4). We would do well, as Ingmire and the rest of *The Saint John's Bible* team have done, to heed the command which immediately follows that promise: "Write this, for these words are trustworthy and true."

Bibliography

Boyle, Nicholas. *Sacred and Secular Scriptures: A Catholic Approach to Literature.* Notre Dame: University of Notre Dame Press, 2005.

22. Ibid., 291.

Carnes, Natalie. *Image and Presence: A Christological Reflection on Iconoclasm and Iconophilia*. Stanford: Stanford University Press, 2018.

Gullick, Michael, and Thomas Ingmire. *Words of Risk: The Art of Thomas Ingmire*. Norman, OK: Calligraphy Review Ed, 1989.

Ingmire, Thomas. *Codici: A Teacher's Notebook on Modern Calligraphy and Lettering Art*. San Francisco: Scriptorium Saint Francis, 2003.

Massironi, Manfredo. "The Pleasure of Showing and Looking at Words." In *Codici: A Teacher's Notebook on Modern Calligraphy and Lettering Art*, 6–17. San Francisco: Scriptorium Saint Francis, 2003.

Nichols, Aidan. *Christendom Awake: On Re-Energising the Church in Culture*. Edinburgh: T. & T. Clark, 2000.

Nixon, Bruce. "Review: The Calligraphy of Thomas Ingmire." http://www.thomasingmire.com/7.html.

———. "Things that Dream" in *Things that Dream: Contemporary Calligraphic Artists' Books* edited by Lorna Price, Kendra Armer, Pam Rino Evans, Diane Roby, and Elizabeth Fischbach, 1–32. Stanford: Stanford University Libraries, 2012.

Patella, Michael. *Word and Image: The Hermeneutics of* The Saint John's Bible. Collegeville, MN: Liturgical, 2013.

Sink, Susan. *The Art of* The Saint John's Bible: *The Complete Reader's Guide*. Collegeville, MN: Liturgical, 2013.

Wilson, Janet. "Where Word and Image Meet—Thomas Ingmire." *Calligraphy Idea Exchange* 2.3 (1984) 16–23.

8

Personal but not Individual

How *The Saint John's Bible* Responds to Consumerism

JEFFREY BILBRO

IF YOU WALK DOWN the Bible aisle in one of the few remaining Christian bookstores, you'll be confronted with a bewildering array of formats and editions. If by some chance they don't have a Bible that appeals to you, you can hop on Amazon.com and use their "Find the Perfect Bible" feature to search among 42,084 options. You might be drawn to the *Busy Dad's Bible: Daily Inspiration Even if You Only Have One Minute*, or to the *Duck Commander Faith and Family Bible*, containing "stories and testimonials" from the stars of the Duck Dynasty television show. If you want a politically-flavored version, you could try the *1599 Geneva Bible: Patriot's Edition*, which includes texts such as The Mayflower Compact and the United States Constitution, or you could get *The Green Bible*, which helpfully highlights environmental passages and inserts "inspirational essays."[1] Your options are limited only by your desires and the size of your wallet.

It's easy to see this proliferation of editions as a symptom of American consumerism. David Jeffrey rightly observes that such "niche editions seem rather to be packaged in such a way as to justify, in some measure, current fashions and practices of the sub-groups to which they are directed. This makes them profitable for the publishers, but not so 'profitable,' at least in

---

1. *Busy Dad's Bible*; NKJV, *Duck Commander Faith and Family Bible*; *1599 Geneva Bible, Patriot's Edition*; *The Green Bible*.

the sense intended by the Apostle, for the Church."[2] Yet while we should certainly critique the crass commercialism these Bibles embody, there may be a seed of genuine theological insight within such efforts to make the Bible more personal. Indeed, faith communities found ways to personalize the divine revelation long before the age of print and consumerism, and the community at Saint John's Abbey has creatively reimagined what such practices might look like in our day. In the essay that follows, I argue that *The Saint John's Bible* recovers a medieval sense of God's revelation as a personal word without succumbing to the consumerist temptations of our contemporary culture. It does so by portraying the Bible as both personal and communal, both local and catholic, both contemporary and ancient.[3] By holding these apparent opposites together, it reminds us that the Bible is a word to us personally, but not to us individually; it does not accommodate its message to our preexisting desires and expectations; rather, it accommodates us to its revelation.

The root problem with these niche Bibles is not *that* they make the Bible personal, but *how* they do so. They tame the Bible, making it a therapeutic consumable: the Bible becomes another fashion accessory, an indicator of the social club to which I belong, just one more object I purchase to shape and express my individual identity. In some ways, this sense of the Bible as a private text that belongs to the individual reader to handle and read and interpret on his or her own is a natural outworking of print technology. Printing made Bibles affordable, contributing to both democracy and consumerism, and the resulting sense of the Bible as a private possession has far-reaching consequences.[4] Thomas Jefferson's *The Life and Morals of Jesus of Nazareth*, commonly known as "The Jefferson Bible," exemplifies some of the dangers involved in viewing the Bible this way. Jefferson cut up six different copies of the Bible and pasted the fragments together to form an account of Jesus' life that he could rationally accept.[5] Jefferson's mode of constructing his own Bible follows the same solipsistic

2. Jeffrey, "Our Babel of Bibles: Scripture, Translation, and the Possibility of Spiritual Understanding."

3. William Cavanaugh offers a thoroughgoing critique of consumerism in similar terms, emphasizing Christianity's insistence on the local and catholic, the personal and communal, in *Being Consumed*.

4. Eisenstein, *The Printing Press as an Agent of Change*; Ong, *Ramus, Method, and the Decay of Dialogue*; Noll, *America's God*; Hatch, *The Democratization of American Christianity*; Marsden, "Everyone One's Own Interpreter?"

5. "The Jefferson Bible."

hermeneutic that Nathaniel Hawthorne critiques in his story "The Man of Adamant," in which the protagonist takes his Bible and his gun off to a wilderness cave and insists on reading his Bible all by himself. As he reads in the dark cave, "he made continual mistakes . . . , converting all that was gracious and merciful, to denunciations of vengeance and unutterable woe, on every created being but himself."[6] The result is that he turns into a petrified statue, frozen in place with his book. While these Bibles don't sport trendy covers, and while *The Busy Dad's Bible* doesn't alter the biblical text, they all belong to the same lineage, one that changes God's self-revelation to fit our lives rather than changing our lives to fit it.

Nevertheless, the individualized Bibles of both Thomas Jefferson and the contemporary American consumer are best understood not as an aberration from the Christian gospel, but a distortion of its startlingly personal address. So while one response to this warped, solipsistic inwardness is to emphasize abstract doctrine and objective logic, a better approach, according to Charles Taylor, is to recover the genuinely dialogical nature of Christian personhood—the person embedded in community with others and with God. Taylor traces the "subjective turn of modern culture" to Christianity itself, particularly as articulated by Saint Augustine. Modern notions of "inwardness, in which we come to think of ourselves as beings with inner depths," Taylor argues, "can be seen just as a continuation and intensification of the development inaugurated by Saint Augustine, who saw the road to God as passing through our own reflexive awareness of ourselves."[7] Taylor describes this movement through the words of Étienne Gilson: "Augustine's path is one 'leading from the exterior to the interior and from the interior to the superior.'" Hence for Augustine "we come to God within."[8] Because the Creator God of the universe became an incarnate baby in a Bethlehem manger, because he surrounded himself with a motley band of fishermen and tax collectors and women, because he told these followers that "the kingdom of God is within you," because of the psychological complexity revealed in his disciples' testimonies, the spread of Christianity led to the development of a newly expansive, interior self.[9]

6. Hawthorne, *The Snow Image and Uncollected Tales*, XI:166.

7. Taylor, *The Ethics of Authenticity*, 26–27.

8. Taylor, *Sources of the Self*, 136.

9. Luke 17:21, KJV. In addition to Taylor's *Sources of the Self*, see Erich Auerbach's incisive analysis of figural realism, which also pivots on Augustine, in *Mimesis*.

The problem, of course, is that for many thinkers following Augustine, this inward path toward a personal God is truncated and never culminates in the movement toward the "superior," the Creator who is present within us. Taylor identifies Jean-Jacques Rousseau as a pivotal figure in this flattening of the expansive self. Rousseau developed "the notion of what I want to call self-determining freedom. It is the idea that I am free when I decide for myself what concerns me."[10] Such a view of individual freedom battens down the hatches of the expanded self; while Augustine explores "the fields and vast palaces" of his mind to find God, Rousseau's inheritors search for a true, authentic self without reference (supposedly) to God, tradition, or community.[11] The result is what Taylor elsewhere describes as a "buffered self," insulated from spiritual influences.[12] Hence the Romantic ideal of the isolated artist, "an agent of original self-definition," becomes the paradigmatic individual.[13] This understanding of the self undergirds our contemporary consumerism, narcissism, and individualism, our obsession with self-actualization, self-expression, and authenticity.[14]

Taylor argues, however, that rather than simply bemoaning such a debased view of the self, or seeking to return to some previous condition, we should work to rehabilitate the Christian gift of authentic personhood. He acknowledges that "there are dangers" inherent in an expanded, interior self and that "when we succumb to these, it may be that we fall in some respects below what we would have been had this culture never developed. But at its best authenticity allows a richer mode of existence."[15] It does so by placing great importance on the *response* of each person to the call of God. The Creator of the universe has a call upon your life, and how *you* respond matters. For Taylor, contemporary notions of the self provide an opportunity "to persuade people that self-fulfillment, so far from excluding unconditional relationships and moral demands beyond the self, actually requires these in some form."[16] Or as he puts it elsewhere, "To shut out

10. Taylor, *The Ethics of Authenticity*, 27.

11. Augustine, *Confessions*, 10.12.

12. Taylor, *A Secular Age*, 37–43.

13. Taylor, *The Ethics of Authenticity*, 62.

14. Taylor points to Lasch as one cultural critic who clearly sees the dangers of contemporary notions of the self; see Lasch, *The Culture of Narcissism*. For an excellent theological account of what vocation can mean in this context, see Cavanaugh, "Actually, You *Can't* Be Anything You Want (and It's a Good Thing, Too)."

15. Taylor, *The Ethics of Authenticity*, 74.

16. Ibid., 72–73.

demands emanating beyond the self is precisely to suppress the conditions of significance, and hence to court trivialization."[17] It is this trivialization that David Jeffrey rightly fears consumerist Bibles contribute to. Green people get green Bibles to tell them God cares about the environment. Dads get dad Bibles to tell them God cares about dads. The marketing and formatting of these editions predispose readers to expect that God wants to meet them where they're at so that he can reinforce their previously chosen identity. The very form of these Bibles has a tendency to desensitize readers to the possibility that God's revelation of himself could actually upset their prior sense of purpose and calling and personhood.

The Saint John's Bible, alternatively, offers one form a Bible might take that could shape receptive readers, readers willing to hear an external, divine call that is nonetheless deeply personal. In a culture that is committed to an expansive self with "inward depths" and that is vigilant to resist any outside claims that might infringe on the self's freedom, such a winsome appeal—one based on beauty—holds great promise. This is because beauty is a deeply subjective, interior experience, but it's a subjective experience of an external reality. When I perceive something as beautiful, there is a resonance between my subjective, internal self, and the external, material object I'm sensing. The way Taylor defines authenticity involves precisely this subjective response to an objective standard or call:

> Authenticity is clearly self-referential: this has to be *my* orientation. But this doesn't mean that on another level the *content* must be self-referential: that my goals must express or fulfil my desires or aspirations, *as against* something that stands beyond these. I can find fulfilment in God, or a political cause, or tending the earth. Indeed, the argument above suggests that we will find genuine fulfilment only in something like this, which has significance independent of us or our desires.[18]

We need to own the call of God on our lives personally, and experiencing the *beauty* of this call allows us to sense this external content in an interior, and hence authentic, manner. As Rilke's poem testifies, an experience of beauty can lead to the dramatically personal realization that "you must change your life."[19]

17. Ibid., 40.

18. Ibid., 81–82.

19. Rilke, *Selected Poems of Rainer Maria Rilke*, 147. David Jeffrey's trenchant observation in *People of the Book* is also pertinent here: "It is this final centrality of the Person

Shaping the physical form of the Bible so as to emphasize and unfold the intrinsic beauty of God's revelatory address, therefore, primes us to hear God's call in an authentic, personal way. The art of *The Saint John's Bible* can "make certain demands from beyond the self more palpable and real for us." Rather than the coercive demands of "disengaged reason" or the merely self-referential void of "subjective fulfillment," its beauty invites a subjective response to an external reality.[20] In responding to beauty's personal invitation, our very selves—in all their inward depths—are re-arranged and aligned to the order of God's revelation.[21] As Hans Urs von Balthasar argues, beauty is essential in teaching us how to pray and love; beauty draws out our deepest desires and affections, ordering them toward their proper end in the God who made us and dwells within us.[22]

Because of beauty's particular power, Christian communities have long worked to make Bibles beautiful in ways that would prime readers to experience God's revelation as a personal, relational word. Some monastic communities—like those at Iona who produced *The Book of Kells*, or those on the isle of Lindisfarne who produced the *Lindisfarne Gospels*—transcribed and illuminated their own Bibles using locally-adapted scripts and art forms. These Bibles were often further adapted to local needs in other ways; several centuries after their creation, for instance, knowledge of Latin was declining, so Aldred added an Old English gloss between the lines of the *Lindisfarne Gospels*.[23] And in Bibles that included the *Glossa ordinaria*, scribes often interspersed the standard Gloss with additional commentary deemed suitable for particular purposes and communities.[24]

Another way that medievals shaped Bibles, as well as other religious art, to emphasize the personal address of God's revelation was by including images of local patrons alongside the biblical narrative. Admittedly, patrons often demanded such recognition in exchange for their sponsorship, so like the niche Bibles of today, this form of personalization was also warped by

---

which, in a world of imperfect speech and imperfect deeds, makes *metanoia* rather than *gnosis* the redemptive goal of" both scripture and all human language. Jeffrey, *People of the Book*, 378.

20. Taylor, *The Ethics of Authenticity*, 90–91.

21. On the way that Christ's beauty tunes hearts that are warped and damaged by sin, see von Balthasar, *The Glory of the Lord*, 463–67.

22. Ibid., 18.

23. Henry, *The Book of Kells*; Brown, *The Lindisfarne Gospels and the Early Medieval World*.

24. Smith, *The Glossa Ordinaria*, 73–76.

political and economic realities.[25] The *Bible of Saint Louis*, a *bible moralisée*, serves as an instructive example. It contains an illumination that appears to show the queen mother instructing a young King Louis IX. This relationship is paralleled below where a cleric on the left instructs the scribe's work on the manuscript. These forms of personal address prepare the king to see the book's biblical texts and illuminations as similarly intended for his instruction (the political implications are also clear—this is not a republican Bible). Yet it represents the young king as accountable to his broader community—particularly his mother and church authorities—so that while the Bible's message is personal, it is not a private possession for him to read however he pleases.[26] The revealed word is for *you*, but it's a word that is heard and responded to in community.

Even as the printing press made Bibles more affordable, as well as more fungible and impersonal, communities still found ways to make the Bible's personal appeal tangible. Many large family bibles left blank pages between the Old and New Testaments for families to record their genealogies and baptismal records.[27] Family members came to know their identity within the context of the biblical narrative. But rather than its authors (as Jefferson's Bible implied), its possessors (as Hawthorne's Man of Adamant believed) or its consumers (as niche Bibles suggest), we are members enfolded into a grand narrative that stretches from the beginning of creation to its eschaton and that makes sense of our lives and local histories.

The Saint John's Bible continues in this tradition, employing aesthetic forms that disclose the personal nature of God's address. From before readers even open the cover of the first volume, all the way to the culminating vision of Revelation, its pages put readers on notice that the words recorded here bear a transformative challenge directed to the "inward depths" of each person—those with ears to hear and eyes to see will find themselves confronted by a beauty that requires them to change their lives. The Bible's size, its treatment of the text, and its many illuminations work together to convey the sense that the biblical revelation is both personal and communal, local and catholic, contemporary and ancient.

The first thing one notices about *The Saint John's Bible* is its size. While the original hasn't yet been bound, some of the seven volumes will weigh as much as 35 pounds, and when held open, the pages measure approximately

25. See, for example, Tilghman, "The Tradition of Giant Medieval Bibles," 63–65.
26. Lowden, *The Making of the* Bibles Moralisées, 127–32.
27. Jeffrey and Maillet, *Christianity and Literature*, 108–9.

three-feet wide and two-feet tall. This is not a book that you can curl up with on your La-Z-Boy or take with you to your cave in the woods; it invites us to read alongside others, whether in a formal liturgical setting or as the center of a conversation with a handful of participants. Other features mark it as a text intended for a particular, Benedictine community. For instance, a small black cross appears in the margin next to verses that are quoted in *The Rule of Saint Benedict*.[28] And several of the texts chosen for special treatment are ones used in the Benedictine liturgy for particular services.[29] These features, along with its size, serve as reminders that this book bears witness to a specific, worshiping community.

There are further indications of an even more intimate address, an address heard within the context of a community but directed toward individuals. On the penultimate page of the Bible, an illumination represents the New Jerusalem (see Figure 14, *Vision of the New Jerusalem*). At the bottom right corner are two gold crosses. When the manuscript was completed, it was brought to the Abbey Church in Collegeville, and during an evening service, the Abbot of Saint John's Abbey and the President of Saint John's University each burnished one of these crosses. Yet even after this ceremony of dedication, Donald Jackson remained dissatisfied with the image, convinced that something was lacking. While working on the Heritage Edition, he added varicolored squares and triangles along the bottom margin to represent the ingathering of every tribe and nation.[30] He then had to return to Saint John's Abbey and reproduce this design for the original manuscript.[31] Besides being an interesting story, one that unsettles the relationship between the original manuscript and its reproductions, Jackson's addition makes an important theological point about the nature of Christian community. The two gold crosses representing the leaders of the Saint John's community retain their individual place in the grand procession entering the New Jerusalem, but they are now joined by the great community of saints. In this way, the illumination testifies that God's redemption is for all people, and yet it is also deeply personal; it is catholic (in the sense of "universal") and yet it is for particular individuals.

28. Sink, *The Art of* The Saint John's Bible, 24, 116.

29. Patella, *Word and Image*, 101, 248.

30. His use of multicolored squares and triangles here was inspired by an illumination Hazel Dolby did in Nehemiah 8 to indicate the scattered people of Israel.

31. Jackson, *The Saint John's Bible*.

The Saint John's Bible consistently conveys this sense of a personal, particular revelation embedded in a broader, universal one. The Benedictine monks of Saint John's Abbey regularly chant the psalms as part of the Divine Office, and they found a beautiful way to honor this liturgical context in the book of Psalms. Running across the pages of the Psalms are gold patterns derived from "oscilloscopic voiceprints of the monks of Saint John's Abbey chanting at prayer."[32] On the frontispiece of the Psalms, where this gold pattern is most clearly rendered, other voiceprints run vertically through the five scrolls representing the five books of the Psalms. These are chant prints from "Jewish, Native American, Taoist, Hindu Bhajan, Greek Orthodox, Muslim, and Buddhist Tantric traditions."[33] Michael Patella, who served as the chair of the Committee on Illumination and Text for *The Saint John's Bible*, explains that these crossing chant lines testify to God's universal self-revelation: "God is Lord of creation, and all creation reflects his truth and goodness. The church always rejoices in truth wherever it may be found."[34] The Christian tradition voiced by the monks in chanting these Psalms is both akin to and yet radically unique from these other religious traditions. In its mode of illuminating the Psalms, then, *The Saint John's Bible* differentiates between the special revelation found here and the general revelation found elsewhere, while still honoring the validity of both revelations.

One very mundane way that this Bible emphasizes its particular, local roots is through the flora and fauna that grace its pages. Almost all of the creatures represented are inhabitants of either Minnesota, where Saint John's Abbey is located, or Wales, where Donald Jackson's scriptorium is situated.[35] They are not just generic representatives of the Book of Nature; they are members of the specific communities where this Bible originated. One paradigmatic example appears at the end of Mark. Alongside the account of Christ's resurrection is a vivid image of a milkweed plant with a monarch caterpillar, a chrysalis, and four butterflies (see Figure 7, *Milkweed and Butterfly*). While the monarch's entire lifecycle is depicted—suggesting a parallel between the resurrection and the insect's dramatic metamorphosis—the milkweed leaves are curled and browning. This is not just any milkweed plant; it is one growing in the northern United States—

32. Sink, *The Art of* The Saint John's Bible, 149.

33. Ibid., 155.

34. *Word and Image*, 193.

35. Sink, *The Art of* The Saint John's Bible, 12.

namely, Minnesota—where monarchs breed in the late summer before the great-great-grandchildren of the previous winter's migrants make the long trek south. The resurrection, and the regeneration it promises to a groaning creation, is for this plant, these butterflies.

In the same way that *The Saint John's Bible* situates its personal address within a larger community, and gives a local accent to its universal context, it also reminds readers that while the biblical word is ancient, it continues to speak today. There are many illuminations I could point to that use modern-day images to suggest ways in which these texts remain vibrant many generations after they were written: the farmer in the image of the sower sowing seed is wearing jeans and a sweatshirt while his face appears in the style of Eastern iconography; the illumination of Ezekiel's dry bones contains images from several twentieth-century genocides; the menorah with Jesus' family tree includes double helix strands of DNA; the twin towers of the World Trade Center appear within the *Luke Anthology* next to the father welcoming home the prodigal son (see Figure 8, *Luke Anthology*). Again and again *The Saint John's Bible* testifies that these words that have spoken to the faithful for millennia speak to us now as well.

One illumination that conveys the divine word's ongoing life with particular insight appears at the end of Romans 8 (see Figure 13, *Fulfillment of Creation*). The bottom of this image harkens back to the first panel in Genesis that represents the seven days of creation. Near the top is an astronomical image adapted from a photo taken by the Hubble telescope.[36] The image includes text drawn from Romans 8, emphasizing Paul's claim that nothing "in all creation" "will separate us from the love of Christ." Around these fragments of text swirl chunks of binary code, plot marks and graphs, and mathematical formulae. Our digital technologies and the equations we use to understand the physical properties of creation and to accomplish the modern engineering marvels of space exploration are all forms of sub-creation. As such, they too can unfold the pattern of divine love that was spoken into being in Genesis and recapitulated in the incarnate and redeeming Word of Christ. We might think that the binary language on which computers run is utterly alien to the Word of God, but this illumination suggests that the God "who searches the heart," the Spirit who knows us so intimately that he can convey our wordless prayers, can speak the language of our modern technologies.[37] God's love remains present in our

36. Ibid., 293.
37. Romans 8:26–27.

digital age; it is for us. And this deeply intimate, contemporary love is the same love that spoke the universe into being.

This mode of illuminating the Bible, a mode that unites the personal and communal, the local and catholic, the contemporary and ancient, bears witness to a divine revelation that is not merely a disembodied, abstract word for everyone everywhere. Instead, it is a word for this people in this place at this time. It is an eternal word that is nevertheless spoken for you, right here and right now. Yet while this word is for you, it is not a word that you can cut apart and rearrange to suit your individual preferences; it's not a word you can easily adapt to the cultural sub-group with which you identify; it's not a word you can read by yourself in a cave. Rather, it's a Word whose personal address cuts you apart—laying bare the "thoughts and intentions of the heart"—and invites you into the eternal, catholic community of those who have responded faithfully to its call.[38]

One final illumination may bring the significance of this aesthetic mode into sharper focus. To better appreciate its import, however, I want to reflect briefly on the word *illumination* itself. Donald Jackson defines illumination as "the play of light on gold," and indeed when you turn the pages of this Bible, the reflective texture of the gold leaf appears to cast light outward.[39] In this way, the illuminations in *The Saint John's Bible* invert the orientation of light that we generally imagine when we read a print text—the light seems to flow outward from the page to the reader. The illuminations attest to the light-giving power inherent in the words of revelation themselves.

This light-giving power is one of the defining features of the divine Word. God's first word in Genesis 1 is "Let there be light," and the psalmist testifies accordingly, "Your word is a lamp to my feet and a light to my path."[40] And John declares about the incarnate Word, "The light shines in the darkness, and the darkness did not overcome it. . . . The true light, which enlightens everyone, was coming into the world."[41] Later, John simply states that "God is light."[42] God's Word—both the second person of the Trinity and the written scripture whose authority depends on this original

---

38. Hebrews 4:12.

39. Bruner, "New Embossing Techniques in the *Gospels and Acts* Volume."

40. Genesis 1:3; Psalms 119:105.

41. John 1:5, 9.

42. 1 John 1:5.

Word—illuminates the world and our understanding. Apart from this revelation, we dwell in darkness.

Why am I belaboring this point? Because as the extensive, interior self, a self with inward depths, developed in the Romantic period, a primary metaphor used to understand the mind shifted. Instead of imagining the self as a mirror that responds to the light of the world, Romantic artists began to imagine the self as a lamp that originates its own meaning. As W. B. Yeats famously declared, the "soul must become its own betrayer, its own deliverer, the one activity, the mirror turn lamp."[43] What's at stake here is the source of meaning, whether the external world or the interior subject. As M. H. Abrams puts it in his seminal work *The Mirror and the Lamp*, Yeats's contrasting images identify "two common and antithetic metaphors of mind, one comparing the mind to a reflector of external objects, the other to a radiant projector which makes a contribution to the object it perceives."[44] Those who imagine the mind as its own lamp are prone to appropriate God's word for their own purposes, cutting it up or slapping trendy covers on it. But in the gold and silver illuminations of *The Saint John's Bible*, the written word of God shimmers with reminders of its divine origin, its source in the one who declared "Let there be light."

The illumination at the end of the gospel of John depicts Mary Magdalene's encounter with this light-giving Word (see Figure 11, *Resurrection*). According to John, when Mary first sees the resurrected Jesus, she mistakes him for the gardener and asks him where he has taken Jesus' body. Jesus replies by simply stating her name, "Mary." He knows her personally. Suddenly enlightened, Mary responds with the word for teacher, "Rabbouni!" In the illumination, this word appears in Aramaic next to the figure of Mary. Jesus has his back toward us, and Mary's face acts as the mirror in which we see the transformative power of the resurrected Christ. As she reaches her hand toward him, it becomes transparent, revealed and laid bare in the light of his glorified countenance. This scene dramatizes an external yet personal call, and a faithful, subjective response. Mary models for us what happens when we come face-to-face with the Word of God. And in an analogous way, when we read the written words of Scripture, we are likewise read, interpreted, transformed, and found out. We are not the illuminating subject but the illuminated object, receiving our subjectivity as a gift. This is the personal word that the beauty of *The Saint John's Bible*

43. Yeats, "Introduction," xxxiii.
44. Abrams, *The Mirror and the Lamp*, viii.

manifests for its readers, a word that reaches into the core of our being, reshaping our lives in response to its intimate address.

Bibliography

1599 Geneva Bible: Patriot's Edition. 2nd ed. Sandersville, GA: White Hall, 2012.

Abrams, Meyer Howard. *The Mirror and the Lamp: Romantic Theory and the Critical Tradition.* Oxford: Oxford University Press, 1971.

Auerbach, Erich. *Mimesis: The Representation of Reality in Western Literature.* Translated by Willard R. Trask. 1953. Reprint, Princeton Classics. Princeton: Princeton University Press, 2013.

Augustine. *Confessions.* Translated by Henry Chadwick. Oxford: Oxford University Press, 1998.

Balthasar, Hans Urs von. *Seeing the Form.* The Glory of the Lord: A Theological Aesthetics 1. Translated by Erasmo Leiva-Merikakis. Edited by Joseph Fessio and John Riches. San Francisco: Ignatius, 1982.

Brown, Michelle. *The Lindisfarne Gospels and the Early Medieval World.* London: British Library, 2011.

Bruner, Craig. "New Embossing Techniques in the *Gospels and Acts* Volume." *The Scribe* (Winter 2012).

Busy Dad's Bible: Daily Inspiration Even If You Only Have One Minute. Grand Rapids: Zondervan, 2010.

Cavanaugh, William T. "Actually, You *Can't* Be Anything You Want (and It's a Good Thing, Too)." In *Field Hospital: The Church's Engagement with a Wounded World,* 74–98. Grand Rapids: Eerdmans, 2016.

———. *Being Consumed: Economics and Christian Desire.* Grand Rapids: Eerdmans, 2008.

Eisenstein, Elizabeth L. *The Printing Press as an Agent of Change: Communications and Cultural Transformations in Early Modern Europe.* 2 vols. Cambridge: Cambridge University Press, 1979.

The Green Bible. San Francisco: HarperOne, 2008.

Hatch, Nathan O. *The Democratization of American Christianity.* New Haven: Yale University Press, 1989.

Hawthorne, Nathaniel. *The Snow Image and Uncollected Tales.* Vol. 11. Centenary Edition. 23 vols. Columbus: Ohio State University Press, 1974.

Henry, Françoise, ed. *The Book of Kells: Reproductions from the Manuscript in Trinity College, Dublin.* New York: Knopf, 1988.

Jackson, Donald. The Saint John's Bible: *A Contemporary Illuminated Manuscript.* 2012. https://www.youtube.com/watch?v=h239XcNGq94.

"The Jefferson Bible." *National Museum of American History, Smithsonian Institution.* http://americanhistory.si.edu/JeffersonBible/the-book/.

Jeffrey, David Lyle. "Our Babel of Bibles: Scripture, Translation, and the Possibility of Spiritual Understanding." *Touchstone Magazine,* 2012. http://www.touchstonemag.com/archives/article.php?id=25-02-029-f.

———. *People of the Book: Christian Identity and Literary Culture.* Grand Rapids: Eerdmans, 1996.

Jeffrey, David L., and Gregory Maillet. *Christianity and Literature: Philosophical Foundations and Critical Practice*. Downers Grove, IL: IVP Academic, 2011.

Lasch, Christopher. *The Culture of Narcissism: American Life in an Age of Diminishing Expectations*. New York: Norton, 1991.

Lowden, John. *The Making of the* Bibles Moralisées. Vol. 1. 2 vols. University Park: Pennsylvania State University Press, 2000.

Marsden, George M. "Everyone One's Own Interpreter?: The Bible, Science, and Authority in Mid-Nineteenth Century America." In *The Bible in America: Essays in Cultural History*, edited by Nathan O. Hatch and Mark A. Noll, 79–100. New York: Oxford University Press, 1982.

NKJV, Duck Commander Faith and Family Bible. Edited by Phil and Al Robertson. Signature. Nashville: Nelson, 2014.

Noll, Mark A. *America's God: From Jonathan Edwards to Abraham Lincoln*. Oxford: Oxford University Press, 2002.

Ong, Walter J. *Ramus, Method, and the Decay of Dialogue: From the Art of Discourse to the Art of Reason*. Chicago: University of Chicago Press, 2004.

Patella, Michael. *Word and Image: The Hermeneutics of* The Saint John's Bible. Collegeville, MN: Liturgical, 2013.

Rilke, Rainer Maria. *Selected Poems of Rainer Maria Rilke*. Translated by Robert Bly. New York: Harper & Row, 1981.

Sink, Susan. *The Art of* The Saint John's Bible: *The Complete Reader's Guide*. Collegeville, MN: Liturgical, 2013.

Smith, Lesley. *The Glossa Ordinaria: The Making of a Medieval Bible Commentary*. Commentaria 3. Leiden: Brill, 2009.

Taylor, Charles. *A Secular Age*. Cambridge: Belknap, 2007.

———. *Sources of the Self: The Making of the Modern Identity*. Cambridge: Harvard University Press, 1989.

———. *The Ethics of Authenticity*. Cambridge: Harvard University Press, 1991.

Tilghman, Benjamin C. "The Tradition of Giant Medieval Bibles." In *Word and Image: The Hermeneutics of* The Saint John's Bible, 51–70. Collegeville, MN: Liturgical, 2013.

Yeats, W. B. "Introduction." In *The Oxford Book of Modern Verse*, edited by W. B. Yeats. New York: Oxford University Press, 1936.

9

The Social Conscience of
The Saint John's Bible

PAUL N. ANDERSON

ONE OF THE AMAZING features of the striking new artwork in *The Saint John's Bible* is the way that so many of its images capture the social concerns of biblical texts in ways that speak to twenty-first-century issues in gripping and prophetic ways. Especially powerful are the ways the artwork in these seven volumes addresses issues related to women, ecology, globalization, violence, poverty, wellbeing, healing, and redemption. As historic artistic contributions to society in the new millennium, many of its 160 pieces of art thus speak powerfully to contemporary issues in ways that convey timeless truths in timely ways. Tolstoy described the highest value of great art as its religious or spiritual power to speak to the issues of the day, and that being the case, the new artwork in these seven volumes are destined to be classics from the start. In that sense, the social conscience of *The Saint John's Bible* speaks powerfully, engaging culture with prophetic confrontation and spiritual illumination.[1]

---

1. For a helpful guide to the background of each of the artistic pieces in *The Saint John's Bible*, see Susan Sink, *The Art of* The Saint John's Bible; for a guide to the process behind the project, see Christopher Calderhead, *Illuminating the Word: The Making of* The Saint John's Bible. Earlier drafts of these essays were posted on my *Huffington Post* page in 2015–2016: http://www.huffingtonpost.com/author/panderso-792, and the final three essays below are subtitled "The Social Conscience of *The Saint John's Bible* I, II, and III."

"A Mission of Love"—Seven Features over Seven Days

Rather than focus on one or two paintings in particular, this essay will comment on several key paintings, beginning with seven paintings that were featured daily in "A Mission of Love" to America, led by Pope Francis, September 21–27, 2015. In what was designed to celebrate the historic mission of Pope Francis to America, the leaders of the Saint John's University and Abby in Minnesota selected seven pieces of art in Volumes 1 and 6, and over sixty Churches, Colleges, and Universities around the nation featured these texts and their artwork daily in their local settings. A high point of the week involved the giving an Apostles Edition of *The Saint John's Bible* to the Library of Congress on September 24th, celebrated by Pope Francis and leaders of Congress.

In an era where "cultured despisers of religion" fail to note the power and feeling of authentic faith and practice, the mission of Pope Francis to America came at a pivotal moment in world history.[2] As the first Pope of the Americas, his mission to Cuba and the United States called for justice, reconciliation, and grace. His "Mission of Love" embraced the poor, prisoners, and even members of Congress and the White House. As media covered these events, a new day of appreciation for what it means to embrace the way of Jesus touched the hearts and conscience of the nation, focusing on illuminated texts and images from *The Saint John's Bible*, ranging from *Creation* to *Pentecost*. A particular painting and text was featured each day that week:

- Monday (9/21) *Creation* (*Pentateuch*, Vol. 1—Genesis 1:1—2:4a)
- Tuesday (9/22) *Abraham and Sarah* (*Pentateuch*, Vol. 1—Genesis 15:1–7; 17:1–22)
- Wednesday (9/23) *Ten Commandments* (*Pentateuch*, Vol. 1—Exodus 20:1–26)
- Thursday (9/24) *Peter's Confession* (*Gospels & Acts*, Vol. 6—Matthew 16:13–23)
- Friday (9/25) *Multiplication of the Loaves and Fishes* (*Gospels & Acts*, Vol. 6—Mark 6:33–44; 8:1–10)
- Saturday (9/26) *Two Cures* (*Gospels & Acts*, Vol. 6—Mark 5:25–43)

2. A term coined by Friedrich Schleiermacher two centuries ago, critiquing the prevailing ethos of Europe during his day, the thrust is still relevant today; see *On Religion: Speeches to Its Cultured Despisers*.

- Sunday (9/27) *Pentecost* (*Gospels & Acts*, Vol. 6—Acts 1:6–11, 2:1–47)

Creation: Illuminating the Cosmos

As the frontispiece of Volume 1 of *The Saint John's Bible*, Donald Jackson's beautiful painting of *Creation* sets the stage for the entire seven-volume set (see Figure 1, *Creation*). God is the Ground and Source of our being, and at the end of each creative work, "God saw that it was good." Striking against the ancient view that order is achieved through violence and domination, the God of the Hebrews creates and orders the cosmos simply and powerfully by his word. Humans are also created in the divine image, and they are invited into partnership with God in caring for and cultivating the earth. On the seventh day God rested, and in her "Reflection on Creation," Barbara Sutton invites us to consider how to create the space to honor and worship the Creator amidst the business of life.[3]

As the viewer embraces the first piece of art in this amazing collection, the seven days of creation are outlined in seven columns, elucidating each of the seven days mentioned in Genesis 1:1–2:4a. Before the first day, the cosmos was "a formless void" (*tohu wabohu* in the Hebrew language), characterizing the chaos into which God declared, "Let there be light!" A thin ribbon of gold marks the transition from darkness to illumination on that first day. The second day marks the expanse of sky above the waters, and the third day marks the separation of the waters and the land, allowing vegetation to grow. An image of the Ganges River and Delta in India is featured here, which, with its tendencies to flood during monsoon seasons, reminds us of the importance of that separation. Day four features the sun and the moon, ruling day and night and seasons, and teeming creatures of the sea are created on the fifth day. On the sixth day, land animals are created, and humans are here depicted, patterned after aboriginal cave-art drawings of Australia. Here, the female is the hunter, and the coral snake is shown at the bottom of the column, prefiguring the second creation narrative in Genesis 2 and 3. After looking over the creation of humans, "God saw that it was very good!"

On the seventh day God rested, and this column is presented as golden—conveying the fullness of divine presence. If the Creator God was able to rest on the seventh day, so are all of God's children invited into that weekly rest and worship. In ascending number, small squares of embossed

---

3. Sutton, "Illuminating the Mission: A Reflection on Creation."

gold rise from each of the days in Donald Jackson's painting, until the seventh day concludes with seven markers of illumination, typifying the divine presence. We live in a world where constant activity is too often the norm. We run from one event to another, arriving at a new place before our minds and hearts are able to let go of what we were doing or where we were. We pass through life and do not allow ourselves to experience deeply or to be touched by other people. We are in need of soul-searching. We must learn to embrace again love, compassion, and honor for the healing and cultivation of the earth. Embracing the light of the divine presence and restoring harmony to creation become the hallmarks of God's Sabbath rest into which all of humanity is welcomed.

The seven days of creation featured in this painting are also repeated in other artwork throughout the seven volumes, introducing a bit of interfluentiality. In "Garden of Eden" the seven days of creation are featured at the top of the painting, showing how God's creative work flows down into the paradisal garden, even into its fallen state. A second replaying of the seven days is featured in the first and second of the four panels in *Creation, Covenant, Shekinah, Kingdom*, expanding on chapters 10–11 of the deuterocanonical Wisdom of Solomon. Echoing Proverbs 8:22–31, God's wisdom is seen as not only playing a role in the creation of the world, but it also was instrumental in the redemptive history of the people of Israel. The *Covenant* panel then features a white dove bearing an olive branch, echoing the black raven flying across the seven days of creation, introducing the promise of peace to the message-bearing work of the raven. The *Fulfillment of Creation* in Romans 8 also references this image, reminding us that creation has been groaning for the revelation of the adopted children of God, and that nothing can separate us from the love of Christ (see Figure 13, *Fulfillment of Creation*). From the beginning of time to the present day, God's creative-redemptive work not only reminds us whence we've come; it also directs our paths toward a hopeful future.

If the seven days of creation inspire reflection on God's handiwork and love for the world, focusing on the artwork of *The Saint John's Bible* can inspire an embrace of the mission of love that is celebrated today. In addition to being heard, sometimes the Word of God deserves to be seen. After all, it is not only the embossed gold and platinum leaf on the artwork of the page that represents the divine presence, but wherever God's truth and love are conveyed and received, illumination genuinely happens . . . in our lives. That is a reality worth celebrating and embracing; indeed, it is Good News for the world!

Abraham and Sarah: The Blessing of the World

God makes several promises of blessing to Abraham in Genesis 12–17, and these also involve Sarah, extending further to the world. The opening promise in Genesis 12:1–3 involves leaving the familiarity of home and traveling to an unknown land to be shown later. That must have taken courage! Another promise follows in 15:1–6, where despite Abraham's childlessness, God promises to multiply his descendants as numerous as the stars of the sky. That must have taken faith! Yet another promise, in 17:1–22, affirms that Abraham will be the father of many, and the children of both Sarah and Hagar—Isaac and Ishmael—also become the fathers of great nations. That must have involved perseverance!

In this painting by Donald Jackson, the Jewish Menorah[4] is used to anticipate the ways the families of Abraham will be a blessing to the world. From Abraham to Isaac to Jacob to the twelve tribes of Israel and beyond, the family lines of Abraham are set against the innumerable stars of the heavens—reminiscent of outer space photographs taken by the Hubble Telescope. The image of the Menorah is also replicated in depictions elsewhere of the Tree of Life in the Garden of Eden, and it becomes the main feature of the frontispiece of Volume 6, *Gospels and Acts*. In what is the most famous of *The Saint John's Bible* artwork, the Jewish Menorah reflects upon the lineage of Jesus going back to Abraham and Sarah. As a twenty-first-century piece of art, double-helix strands of DNA ornament the candlesticks, set against the firmament of God's creative work. At the bottom right of this painting, the names of Hagar and Ishmael (father of the Arabic nations) are mentioned, and Hagar's name is written in Arabic as well as Hebrew and English. It truly is an interfaith rendering of the Abrahamic promise.

Central to Scripture, thus, is the promise that the children of Abraham will be a blessing to all the families of the earth. The land and the people groups are means to that end, not the end in themselves, and nearly half the world's population is included in the larger families of Abraham: Judaism, Christianity, and Islam. However, therein lies the challenge. Can the families of Abraham really be a blessing to the world instead of a curse? The answer to that question will depend on how the followers of Abraham's God embody

4. A seven-fold candlestick; Exodus 25:31–40.

his love, hospitality, and grace. And, the fulfillment of that promise in the long run hinges upon our courage and faithfulness in the here and now.

Ten Commandments: A Covenant of Love

The Ten Commandments, given to Moses by God for the children of Israel to follow, are not primarily religious. Their concern is largely societal, rooted in love and right living, and all of them are relational in their thrust. The first four Commandments address the human-divine relationship; the remaining six address human-to-human relationships.[5] In this painting by Thomas Ingmire, the various letters of "the ten words" fall from the upper areas of the painting to the lower ones, affecting human realities as they do so (see Figure 2, *Ten Commandments*).

They also move from gold letters and colored images to black and white, reminding us how easy it is for the living Word of God to become reduced to codes of law. And yet, at the top of the painting are four scenarios, reminding readers of momentous events in Israel's salvation history: the burning bush, the first Passover, the sea crossing, and the twelve pillars erected at Mount Sinai. If God was faithful in the past, God can also be trusted for the future.

Within ancient history, though, these calls to covenant faithfulness are not unique. While the codes of Moses and their stipulations in Exodus 20–24 deal with general principles and particular applications for the Children of Israel to follow, the codes of the Babylonian King, Hammurabi—centuries earlier, in modern-day Iraq—also addressed over two hundred right ways of being and doing. In the last painting in Volume 1, Moses is presented as looking into the Promised Land, although he is not allowed to enter.[6] In *Death of Moses*, three artists combine their work to make this piece poignant and powerful. Aidan Hart renders the wistful face of Moses in iconographic form—touching the emotions of the viewer. Donald Jackson portrays the Promised Land and future captivity in Babylon, where the books of Moses were finalized. Thomas Ingmire, though, echoes the earlier Ten Commandments painting in his word-art form, showing Moses clutching the tablets whose standards would impact the legal enterprises and societal values of western civilization for millennia to come.

5. Exodus 20:1–16.

6. Deuteronomy 34:1–12.

Throughout the rest of Hebrew Scripture, the Law of Moses is featured centrally as a standard of societal justice, right living, and authentic faith. The Prophets call people to live by the just and honest ways of the Law, and the Priests call people to render fitting sacrifices to the Lord who delivers them and redeems the land. The Laws of Moses were also central to the teachings of Jesus over a thousand years later, as the love of God and the love of neighbor are summarized as the radical heart of the Ten Commandments. In Volume 6 of *The Saint John's Bible,* the double commandments of Jesus are featured in the margins of the first three Gospels.[7] Here Jesus cites Deuteronomy 6:4–5 (the *Shema*—"Hear, Oh Israel . . .") and Leviticus 19:34 as the heart of the Law, emphasizing supremely the love of God and neighbor as the heart of God's best practices for humanity.

Indeed, things do go better when people embrace respectfully the Ground and Source of our Being, and when they love and respect others as they themselves would wish to be treated. However, following the ways of God is not a transaction, like a contract. Rather, faithfulness to the divine Word involves a loving response to the ways of being and doing disclosed by a loving God. Indeed, authenticity, reverence, humility, hospitality, non-violence, faithfulness, honesty, integrity, and dependability have their own rewards, and all of humanity is invited to embrace these values—that things might be well for all of God's children. And, if people would live by these values, how much better off the entire world would be! In that sense, God's ways are offered to humanity as an extension of God's love, and in their embrace, that love and our love for others, are actualized.

Peter's Confession: The Foundational Rock of the Church

Peter's confession in the Gospels marks the turning point in Jesus' ministry. In Mark and Matthew, the setting is Caesarea Philippi—the headwaters of the Jordan River, where a cave descends deep into the earth.[8] On this site at the base of Mount Hermon, conquering foreign armies erected shrines to their pagan gods, claiming the land for their empires. A visitor cannot escape viewing the deep cave on that site, and one can imagine the gates of *Sheol,* or the gateway to the underworld would have been associated with that site contextually. For Jesus to ask, "Who do you say that I am?" in that setting poses a test to his followers. To confess him before

7. Matthew 22:37–40; Mark 12:29–31; Luke 10:27.
8. Mark 8:27–30; Matthew 16:13–19.

competing faiths and powers may indeed exact a price for the believer, as the gift of life inevitably involves the way of the cross.

This striking painting by Donald Jackson features three presentations—something of a triptych. On the right side is a cubist rendering of Peter, the "rock" of the church, reflecting a bit of humor among the designers and artists. In the middle is an image of Jesus, adorned with illuminative gold leaf, signifying the divine presence. Within his halo, however, is the shape of the cross, as a reminder of the cost of his own faithfulness in his mission. To the left is an image of a conquering horse, reminiscent of warring invaders across the centuries. As a means of giving the gates of *Sheol* a contemporary feel, however, the artists have introduced a microscopic image of the AIDS virus at the center of that image. Can there be any more poignant association of suffering and torment among present-day readers of the Bible? And yet, the promise of Christ is that these threats would not prevail, as the power of Christ transcends all adversity.

After Peter's confessing Jesus to be the Christ in the Synoptics, Jesus warns that the Son of Man must suffer and die—to which his followers object. Before Peter's confessing Jesus as the Holy One of God in John, Jesus calls for ingesting the flesh and blood of the suffering Son of Man— at which even some of his disciples abandon him and walk with him no longer.[9] Whether the rock upon which the church stands is the legacy of Peter, the truth of his confession, or its revelatory origin, Jesus reminds us in Matthew 7 that the solid rock upon which to build is faithfully following Jesus. While the cost of discipleship may be dear, the gift of life is always worthy. In the words of the 19-year-old Quaker martyr, James Parnell a few months before his death, "Be willing that self shall suffer for truth, not the truth for self." Against such a foundational rock, the gates of Hades will never prevail.

Loaves and Fishes: An Invitation into Partnership

The only miracle of Jesus in all four Gospels is the Multiplication of the Loaves and Fishes, and Mark and Matthew even include the feeding of the 4,000 as well as the feeding of the 5,000.[10] While Jesus multiplies the loaves and the fishes, his disciples are charged with distributing them to those who are hungry. They also gather up the fragments, so that nothing should be

9. John 6:51–69.

10. Matthew 14:13–21; 15:32–39; Mark 6:30–44; 8:1–10; Luke 9:10–17; John 6:1–15.

wasted. In feeding the hungry of the world, God provides bounty beyond imagination, but he also invites us into partnership. In John 6, a young boy plays a role in the feeding; he offers his lunch for the to Lord transform and multiply in meeting the world's needs. Can we do any less?

When the designers of *The Saint John's Bible* first laid out the text and the artwork, they had allotted a quarter page for the feeding stories. However, when Donald Jackson thought about the surplus of meaning, as well as the surplus of pieces gathered up in the seven and the twelve baskets, he redesigned the pages around Mark 6 and filled both pages with a proliferation of images.[11] Drawing in the Byzantine mosaic from the floor of the Tabgha Church of the Multiplication on the western shore of the Sea of Galilee, the loaves-and-fishes motif surrounds the artwork on these pages. As the Bible speaks of sins of commission and omission, black and white bars are featured in this artwork, reminding us of things we have done and not done in failing the Lord in partnership with him in the feeding of the world.

As people around the world pray for their daily bread, can his followers play a role in those prayers being answered? If the earth could grow and multiply enough food to feed the world, can Jesus' followers find a way to distribute it so that today's multitudes are also fed? We are reminded of such a calling by "A Mission of Love"—the theme of Pope Francis' visit to America—and embracing these texts and artwork inspires its fulfillment.

Two Cures: The Healing of the World

Jesus proclaimed, "The Kingdom of God is at hand!" He delivered the inwardly afflicted and healed the sick. In the Gospel of Mark, Jesus heals lepers, the lame, the blind, and those suffering from other ailments, furthering God's redemptive work in the world. Those touched by the healing hand of Jesus include women: the mother-in-law of Peter, the daughter of Jairus—the Synagogue leader, and the woman with an issue of blood. In Mark 5:25–34, on the way to attending the dying daughter of Jairus, a woman with an incurable bleeding problem touched Jesus and was healed. He felt the power going out of him. After arriving at the home of the sick girl—now reportedly dead, Jesus took her by the hand and declared, *Talitha koum* (Aramaic for "little girl, arise"), which is added to the artwork. She arose, and all were astonished.

---

11. Sink, *The Art of The Saint John's Bible*, 234–35.

In the painting of three scenes from Mark 5, the iconographic style of Adrian Hart here sketches the healing of women in the earliest of the gospels. These three panels are vertically arranged, framed by a border. God's work is sometimes performed as a surprise, along the way to another healing. Whether Jesus is touched or is the one taking the hand of the other, he declares that human faith is a factor in the work of healing. "Your faith has made you well," declares the Markan Jesus. The artists have also added a theme reminiscent of *Elisha and the Six Miracles* in 2 Kings 4–6, "Do not fear; only believe!"

The ministry of Jesus to women is featured again by Adrian Hart, Donald Jackson, and Sally Mae Johnson in their two-panel artwork on the *Woman Taken in Adultery* from John 7:53—8:11. In this iconographic style, the first panel portrays the shaming of the woman in the temple area, where the Law of Moses is being used as a weapon, along with stones. In the second panel, her accusers are gone, the stones are on the ground, and the veil in the temple is drawn, availing access to the divine presence for all. Here we see the move from the woman's desolation to consolation in the liberating ministry of Christ. In sending out his followers to preach, liberate, and heal, Jesus also extends his ministry to the rest of the world in partnership with his friends. And, in so doing, we are all reminded that we exist not for ourselves, but for the healing of the world.

Pentecost: The Empowerment of the Spirit

As Jesus' followers gathered on Pentecost Sunday, 50 days after the Sabbath following his crucifixion, they were startled by rushing winds and tongues of fire. Travelers had come to Jerusalem from all parts of the known world, but an even more amazing thing happened. Despite representing diverse language groups, people were enabled to speak in and to understand unknown languages. Donald Jackson's artwork depicting Pentecost in *The Saint John's Bible* builds knowing connections with that world-changing event two millennia ago and the grounded situation of Saint John's University and Abby[12] (see Figure 12, *Pentecost*).

In addition to wind, fire, and the illuminated presence of the Holy Spirit, details of the Saint John's Abbey Church are featured, connecting the beginning of the church with its continued vitality. With a bit of artistic license, the enthusiasm of a Saint John's University football game is featured

12. Sink, *The Art of The Saint John's Bible*, 272–74.

at the bottom of the painting, connecting the school spirit of a great athletic tradition with the original Pentecost.

Reported in Acts 2 as the outpouring of the Holy Spirit, the event resembles a reversal of the language-confusion inflicted upon arrogant king Nimrod and builders of the Tower of Babel in Genesis 11. Then Peter stood and preached, declaring this to be the fulfillment of the prophecy of Joel 2:28–32. In the last days, God's Spirit would be poured out on young and old, on men and women, on leaders and servants; those calling upon the name of the Lord would be saved. The response to that world-changing event was impressive! Those responding to the gospel that day numbered 3,000, marking the beginning of the church, and he invited them to be baptized.

In addition to receiving visions of how things ought to be, believers met together for table fellowship, worship, and the teaching of the apostles. They pooled their resources together into a commonwealth, and the needs of all were addressed. When the Holy Spirit is poured out upon human-ity, lives change. Not only does empathy and understanding prevail among diverse people groups, but believers also share what they have with those in need. In the outpouring of the Spirit, the blessings of Abraham are ex-tended to all peoples, and the visionary prophecy of Joel is fulfilled.

Ethiopian Lives Matter

Do people share a common humanity, and if so, what is its character? Whereas Genesis 1:1–2:4a calls for setting aside time for worship, renewal, and relationships on a weekly basis, the next two chapters address our shared humanity. Despite being created in the divine image, humans are also fallen. And yet, the rest of the biblical story shows a God who seeks to restore broken relationships, to bring justice to the world, and to welcome God's children into this healing-redeeming work. Two highly suggestive paintings of *The Saint John's Bible* engage the social conscience of today's readers and viewers powerfully, as *Garden of Eden* displays both the beauty and the dangers of the paradisal garden, and *Adam and Eve* presents a cross-cultural image of the originative human couple.

In *Garden of Eden*, Donald Jackson and Chris Tomlin portray graphi-cally the goodness and the perils of the Garden. A beautiful macaw of Co-lombia and Central America overlooks the scene, with prehistoric cave-art figures playing musical instruments and carrying out life's tasks forms the background. At the bottom of the painting, the poisonous-though-beautiful harlequin shrimp reminds us of beauty and danger conjoined; we can be deceived by beauty as well as blessed by it. Tomlin's marginal sketch of the Welsh thistle, on which a lovely butterfly has lighted, likewise conveys the message of the mingled pain and glories of the created world. In the first three paintings, Tomlin has also added the beautiful coral snake—the most beautiful and poisonous of serpents—representing the tempter in the Garden. Echoed also in *Woman and the Dragon*,[13] the final defeat of the serpent prophesied in Genesis 3:15 is signaled by its being severed in the *Adam and Eve* painting, extending hope to humanity, even amidst its trials and temptations.

Adam and Eve: Ethiopian Lives Matter

From the muddy stuff of the earth is humankind formed ("*adam*"—human—is formed from "*adamah*"—clay), and to dusty decomposition shall humans return.[14] Note also that from the beginning, diversity and mutuality are central to the creation of man and woman. While the mother of the living (Eve) is created as a counterpart to the man (Adam), she is also formed out of his side, emphasizing partnership within diversity.[15] This mutuality is displayed in the renderings of *Garden of Eden* and *Adam and Eve* in *The Saint John's Bible*, as the beauty and dangers of the Garden are confronted together by the originative couple, their faces placed side-by-side. Against the backdrop of a platinum-embossed mirror, the viewer also sees one's own reflection, inviting a sense of personal connection with the biblical pair.

Ironically, though, Bible readers often view these historic figures through the lenses of their own cultures, when they are meant to be seen as typological representatives of full humanity—literally. And, in European-Americans' envisioning Adam and Eve as a Caucasian couple, as most groups see them through the lens of their own heredity, we too easily miss the global thrust of these primordial figures. As a correction to these blinders, the social conscience of *The Saint John's Bible* offers us a new and liberating perspective. Rather than presenting Adam and Eve as a northern European couple, they are rendered as members of the Karo tribe

13. Revelation 12.

14. Genesis 2:7; 3:19

15. Genesis 2:21–3:21.

of southwest Ethiopia. And, if our genetic-tracing technologies are correct in identifying Africa as the source of human origins, there may be an anthropological basis for this connection. Additionally, the border for this painting is constructed of indigenous tapestry designs from the Peruvian highlands, effectively globalizing our understandings of Adam and Eve.

I recently heard a story of an elementary-age boy, who upon seeing this painting of *The Saint John's Bible* a couple of years ago, found tears welling up in his eyes. When someone asked him what he was feeling, he said, "I've never seen myself in the Bible before." He was African-American. While humans were created in the divine image, the fall of humanity is also real, according to Genesis 2–3. This accounts for human capacity for good, as well as humans' afflictions with toil, pain, and social brokenness. And yet, Adam's and Eve's expulsion from the garden of paradise and its fruitfulness raises the question for every generation: How can we get back into that place of ecological harmony and of right relationship with God, with one another, and within ourselves?

In the seventeenth century, George Fox received a vision of entering through the flaming sword back into the place where Adam was before he fell—a gift of God's grace, through the transformative work of the Holy Spirit.[16] In the twentieth century, Martin Luther King, Jr. had a dream of a day when all humanity would be embraced, judged not by the color of their skin, but by the content of their character. And, these are visions worth embracing today! In seeing ourselves in the creation of the first humans—in Ethiopian perspective—perhaps a new sense of righteousness and justice might yet emerge. The Bible was not written in North America; it was written in the Middle East, at the intersection of three continents, challenging provincial perspectives, both then and now. Aided by the social conscience of *The Saint John's Bible*, not only do Ethiopian lives matter, but the lives of all God's children matter, in every age and in every setting.

On Syrian Refugees and the Reversals of Christmas

Pleasant images of nativity scenes adorn hearth and home during Christmas and Advent seasons, but when we stop and take a closer look, our perspectives often change. Upon a closer look, that momentous sojourn in the Levant was more difficult than we might have thought. An unwed pregnant teenager; a forced return to an immigrant's homeland for "tax-registration"

16. Roberts, *Through Flaming Sword*.

purposes; the dislocation of the displaced; the weariness of homeless travelers—this was not a sightseeing excursion! Like Syrian refuges resulting from recent conflicts, and as the followers of the Son of Man would later find, they had no place to lay their heads.

And yet, Luke's story of the birth of Jesus bolsters hope for humanity, not because it offers cookies to midnight visitors or gifts to "nice" children, but because it challenges the bondage of worldly domination and the leveraging of uneven justice. In its graphic presentation of *The Birth of Christ*, the striking artwork of *The Saint John's Bible* exposes several reversals, which pique the social conscience of the modern viewer while also illuminating authentic meanings in the biblical Christmas story.

Birth of Christ: Reversals Then and Now

In the powerful frontispiece of the Gospel of Luke, Donald Jackson notes several reversals that challenge our staid notions of the birth of Jesus on various levels. First, rather than focusing on a baby in a manger, this painting features the manger as an altar table echoed in the painting of the *Life in Community* of the Apostles in Acts 4. The vertical light-beam from heaven, intersected by the illuminating angels, forms the shape of a cross—founded upon the altar/manger as its base. The ram among the animals (echoed in other paintings of Passover sacrifice) brings home the point that the birth of the Christ-child signals his sacrifice on the cross— a poignant destiny, indeed.

Another colorful feature of this painting highlights the images of those coming to see the Christ-child. Mary, Joseph, and the baby are somewhat diminished in their presentation, but the most vivid focus is upon those who have come to see. And, while the biblical text has no mention of a donkey, its inclusion here prefigures Jesus' riding into Jerusalem later, at the end of his ministry, not on a conquering white stallion, but on the humble colt of a donkey. Therefore, a societal reversal is apparent in God's glory being revealed to the humble and lowly—the dispossessed of the land. These are those on whom God's favor is shown.

Speaking of animals, the ox here featured resembles the Neolithic cave art, discovered in Lascaux, France, several decades ago. Thus, even the animals in the manger scene represent a multiplicity of cultures, periods, and associations. This leads into a text quoted from Zechariah's prophecy, that God's tender mercy will "give light to those who sit in darkness in the shadow of death, to guide our feet into the way of peace."[17] The good news of God's saving-revealing work transcends the boundaries of time, place, and culture—bringing liberation to all by the power of grace and truth.

The final irony of this painting, and the biblical text behind it, is that it challenges the political power of Empire and domination with a chorus of angels delivered to lowly shepherds: "Glory to God in the highest heaven, and on earth peace among those whom he favors!"[18] A God who favors the lowly and dispossessed of the land is the God revealed in Luke's birth story—not a projected deity who honors the lords of merchandise, prominence, or power. This message of hope to the lowly and the downtrodden reminds us all of the first priorities of the God revealed in the Christmas story. Love, peace, and light are what the birth of Jesus heralds, and that good news is what this season is all about.

As we consider Syrian travelers and refugees today, as well as the dispossessed of the land across our time-torn world, we cannot help but be reminded of parallels with Mary and Joseph and their difficult situation twenty-one centuries ago. The thrust of Luke's account is not the establishment of one group over another, but a witness to the mercy and grace of God—embracing the downcast and aliens among us, providing refuge and hope for the dispossessed. Sometimes it takes a revelation from on high for our time-bound sensibilities to be reversed, and now as much as ever, we are still in need of the illuminating "dawn of light from on high" to break upon us, by the tender mercy of God.

And, if that happens, we might yet catch a glimpse of the true meaning of the season in ways beyond what we'd imagined. After all, if God's redemptive work privileged dispossessed aliens on the road in years past, might we find ways of yet being open to such reversals in the present? If so, perhaps that would be the greatest reversal of all; merry Christmas!

On Prodigals, Forgiveness, and Honoring 9/11

The Bible is not a safe book! It confronts, disturbs, and challenges as well as being comforting, instructive, and convicting. As arguably the most impactful book in human history, it continues to speak to contemporary audiences—often in ways that surprise us—today and across the centuries. In the early ninth century, the *Book of Kells*, the most famous of

17. Luke 1:79.

18. Luke 2:14.

ancient illuminated Bibles, was produced by Irish monks. They adorned the hand-lettered text of Scripture with hundreds of images and artistic additions, connecting biblical themes with real-life issues. In Michelangelo's day, the Ceiling of the Sistine Chapel rendered in artistic form the highlights of biblical themes in prophetic voice and with creative genius. Now, in the twenty-first century, as the first Benedictine-commissioned illuminated Bible in five and a half centuries has been completed, an artistic and spiritual contribution of similar magnitude and importance to these other great works has been produced. And that work speaks today in ways powerful and convicting.

In addition to the beauty of the calligraphy and the artwork of *The Saint John's Bible*, however, its global impact hinges upon the ways it addresses contemporary issues with a sense of biblical social conscience. Given that the artists have sought to connect the timeless biblical texts with timely issues of the twenty-first century, the engineers of the project have followed the lead of previous masterpieces. Among the most instructive paintings is the *Luke Anthology*, contributed by several artists: Donald Jackson, Sally Mae Joseph and Aidan Hart (see Figure 8, *Luke Anthology*). This painting features key parables in the Gospel of Luke: The Lost Sheep, The Lost Coin, The Lost Son, The Good Samaritan, and Lazarus and Dives, and these representations speak to the social conscience of audiences in three special ways.[19]

Luke Anthology: An Invitation to Forgive

First, in the lower right-hand corner of the painting, the story of poor Lazarus and wealthy Dives is sketched in lucid, provocative ways. As the story goes in Luke 16:19–31, the fortunes of the poor man and the rich man are reversed in the afterlife. Whereas poor Lazarus was hungry and covered with sores in this life, in the next he is comforted in the embrace of Abraham. Whereas the rich man, Dives, had it good in the present life, in the next he is tormented and thirsty, pleading for relief from Lazarus. This is denied, as is the rich man's plea that someone go and warn his five brothers. If they have not heeded the way of Moses and message of the prophets,

19. Sink, *The Art of The Saint John's Bible*, 250–53. In addition to being posted on 9/11 in 2015, it was also posted on Krista Tippett's *On Being* web blog on September 27th, 2015 as "Illuminating the Social Conscience of the Bible's Challenge to Forgive," https://onbeing.org/blog/illuminating-the-social-conscience-of-the-bibles-challenge-to-forgive.

why would a warning from beyond the grave make any difference now? Note how the torment of the rich man, Dives, is illustrated powerfully in this painting, as is the comforting of poor Lazarus in the embrace of father Abraham. If this is what the next world will be like, how might that impact our social awareness and concern in the present?

Second, The Parable of the Good Samaritan in Luke 10:25–37 is referenced, but no images of it are used. Only four sentences are displayed, concluding with a question: "A priest passed by on the other side." "A Levite passed by on the other side." "But a Samaritan was moved to pity and bandaged his wounds." "Which one of these was a neighbor to the man who fell into the hands of robbers?" In looking at this progression, moving diagonally from left to right and bottom to top, it is interesting that no images of people are used. The viewer is thus deprived of limiting any of the characters to a single conception. Priest, Levite, or any other leader, all who neglect the man in need fall short of their neighborly duty. And, whether the helper is a Samaritan or a person of any other ethnic or religious identity, those who show mercy are commended for their neighborly example. Thus, the parable continues to speak as we think about what it means to be an exemplary neighbor within and beyond society's borders.

The third impact of the painting draws together the three parables of Luke 15 in three sketches. With angels hovering around them, a number of hollow coins are accompanied by a silver coin—the one the widow searched for and finally found. And, the lost sheep, sought by the shepherd, stands out against a dark background. The most graphic parable, though, is that of The Prodigal Son. Here the son moves from the pigs he had been reduced to feeding to the embrace of the loving father, whose gracious welcome was undeserved. A coat of many colors is unfurled as a flag, and the story features beautifully the theme of forgiveness and reconciliation. However, as the eye moves diagonally from left to right and from bottom to top, the forgiveness theme makes an abrupt and provocative move. With the application of gold-leaf foil in the form of two Twin Towers, the forgiveness theme strikes home, causing this viewer to swallow hard.

Receiving home a wasteful and ungrateful child is one thing, but for individuals or groups to extend grace following the most murderous terrorist act—the most egregious foreign assault on American soil in our nation's history, save, perhaps Pearl Harbor—poses a prophetic challenge. So, how do we honor the memory of 9/11 without contributing to further atrocities as agents of God's redeeming work? Such is the pointed question *The Saint*

John's Bible raises for its viewers today. Can we find ways to forgive and to love our enemies, especially when the injuries have been severe? That would involve a miracle of grace, but it also might pave the way for miracles of healing and reconciliation in the future, in ways I have not yet imagined. Again, the Bible has never been a safe book; it meddles, confronts, cajoles, and challenges; and yet, it also speaks in ways potentially transformative if we are open to the truth. And, in the hands of Donald Jackson and his associates, the social conscience of this amazing work continues to speak in ways prophetic—on the eleventh of September, and *always*.

Concluding Reflections

As in the day of Friedrich Schleiermacher's Germany over two centuries ago, cultured despisers of religion wrongly regard the content and thrust of the Jewish and Christian Scriptures as religious-only and irrelevant to societies' needs. Such a bias reveals total unawareness with modern biblical scholarship, as today's scholars spend most of their energies exploring historical, political, anthropological, economic, sociological, psychological, folkloric, mythological, linguistic, and contextual features of biblical texts. And, most of the Bible's concerns address issues of conscience within real-life social settings. Thus, it is impossible to view the Bible's messages as irrelevant for contemporary society if the truth of its content is considered thoughtfully and contextually.[20] That's what the powerful artwork of *The Saint John's Bible* enables us to do, as the issues of social conscience it addresses are translated from one context to another. When that happens, not only are we enabled to hear the Word of the Lord; we are empowered to see it.

Bibliography

Anderson, Paul N. *From Crisis to Christ: A Contextual Introduction to the New Testament.* Nashville: Abingdon, 2014.

Calderhead, Christopher. *Illuminating the Word: The Making of* The Saint John's Bible. 2nd ed. Collegeville, MN: The Saint John's Bible, 2015.

Roberts, Arthur. *Through Flaming Sword: The Life and Legacy of George Fox.* Newberg, OR: Barclay, 2008.

20. Anderson, *From Crisis to Christ.*

Schleiermacher, Friedrich. *On Religion: Speeches to Its Cultured Despisers*. Translated and edited by Richard Crouter. Cambridge Texts in the History of Philosophy. Cambridge: Cambridge University Press, 1988.

Sink, Susan. *The Art of* The Saint John's Bible: *The Complete Reader's Guide*. Collegeville, MN: Liturgical, 2013.

Sutton, Barbara. "Illuminating the Mission: A Reflection on Creation." Franciscan Renewal Center, September 21, 2015. https://thecasa.org/2015/09/illuminating-the-mission-day-one-%e2%80%a2-page-one-a-reflection-on-creation/.

10

Musing Dante and Divining Milton

A Collaboration Modeled on *The Saint John's Bible* Project

GRETCHEN BATCHELLER
AND
JANE KELLEY RODEHEFFER

THIS ESSAY IS THE embodiment of a collaboration between students in Pepperdine's second and third course in the Great Books Colloquium and students in both the introductory Painting and intermediate "Explorations in Drawing" courses in the Fine Arts division. This project began as a result of Professor Rodeheffer's desire to develop a project through which my students might enhance their understanding of the visual language in Dante and Milton. What visual cues are embedded in the language of Dante and Milton and how might uncovering them offer students a greater appreciation of the visionary range of narrative and epic poetry? There exists a long tradition of illustrating the *Divine Comedy* and *Paradise Lost* which includes such legendary artists as Sandro Botticelli, William Blake, Auguste Rodin, Gustave Doré, Salvador Dali, and—in our own time—Barry Moser, Sandow Birk, and the African performance artist Mwangi Hutter. In addition, Professor Rodeheffer was aware of *The Saint John's Bible* project as a member of the Board of Overseers of the School of Theology at Saint John's from 2003–2012, during which time much of the Bible was created. What if

155

the unique interpretive matrix that evolved out of the collaboration between the biblical scholars who formed the Committee on Illumination and Text (CIT) at Saint John's and Donald Jackson and the artists at the Scriptorium in Wales could serve as a model for engaging undergraduates in the tradition of illustrating classical texts? Professor Rodeheffer realized that somewhere deep within her pedagogical imagination lay *The Saint John's Bible* project. Perhaps Great Books scholars could be directed to write briefs on carefully selected and visually rich narrative language in the *Inferno* and collaborate with Painting students to create images on canvas.

Toward a Pedagogical Theory for Illuminating Great Texts

To flesh out this idea, Rodeheffer looked to her colleague Gretchen Batcheller, Associate Professor of Painting in the Fine Arts Division at Pepperdine. She soon learned that Professor Batcheller had developed an assignment in her Painting and Drawing courses that required students to work from a narrative, and she was keen to pursue a collaboration in which the Great Books students provided a textual narrative for her students to explore artistically; like the Humanities, art is an intellectual pursuit, and the academic environment offers a unique opportunity to understand, explore, and question the world through discussion, feedback, trial and error, and hands-on experience. Wrestling with input from a variety of sources is a valuable and necessary component in the creative process, insofar as it allows the artist to evolve, grow and transform. At previous institutions, both of us had learned the value, from a liberal arts perspective, of moving across disciplinary and pedagogical boundaries. In developing the collaboration, we drew inspiration from the workshop of Leonardo Da Vinci, which served as a model for innovative ideas; his was a working environment that favored creative and intellectual cross-pollination. As professors at a Christian University, we were also keen to explore classical texts whose narratives followed the Biblical arc of sin, suffering, and redemption, and to engage our students in the wisdom-seeking monastic tradition of *lectio divina*, or sacred reading.

Leonardo Da Vinci was a consummate liberal artist in the original sense of the term: an inventor, painter, scientist, anatomist, engineer, philosopher, architect and sculptor. In late fifteenth- and early sixteenth-century Europe, *ars* (or art) meant something made by human skill and *liberal* meant free.

Although many of Leonardo's inventions would ultimately require the use of the *artes mechanicae* (skills necessary for the creation of artifacts), as Bruce Kimball points out in *Orators & Philosophers: A History of the Idea of Liberal Education,* their use was grounded in the *artes liberales,* the free skills of an educated citizen that were not constrained by or subjugated to skills of production like agriculture, trade, metallurgy, and masonry.[1] The free arts were traditionally associated with the medieval *trivium* and *quadrivium,* although they are currently understood to encompass the humanities, the fine and performing arts, and the social and physical sciences, including mathematics. In terms of the liberal arts, then, our goal was to develop an experiential collaboration focused on the visual imaginations of Dante and Milton—a collaboration meant to inspire *freedom in thinking and creating* in the tradition of the Renaissance workshop.

Leonardo's work spanned a variety of disciplines and platforms, and it reveals the myriad ways in which observation about one area of experience can shed light on a different, seemingly untested area. In leading Great Books students into the environment of an art studio and Art students into the realm of textual analysis, we hoped to loosen the conventional notions of learning that students traditionally rely on. The workshop in which Leonardo apprenticed was a large open space filled with easels, sculptor's turntables, workbenches, kilns and grindstones. His Codex, or bound manuscript, served as an idea file and a source of constant consultation. Leonardo wrote that the purpose of the Codex was "To awaken genius within this jumble of things."

1. Kimball, *Orators and Philosophers.*

In a similar way, Great Books students relied upon Commonplace Books, which were known—in the medieval monastic tradition out of which *The Saint John's Bible* arose—as "books of sparks," their contents based on the ongoing practice of *lectio divina*. In this version of a Codex, students were asked to record and organize important, beautiful, inspiring or quotable passages from each of the classical texts we read, as well as questions, ideas, observations and other information they came across in the course of their learning. In keeping a Commonplace Book, students come to appreciate that reading and writing are inseparable activities. Like the illustration of classical texts, the Commonplace Book also has a long tradition among humanists; indeed, the one kept by Marcus Aurelius ultimately became the *Meditations*, and Montaigne—inventor of the essay—recorded maxims and quotations from literature and history that formed the basis of his earliest *Essais*. Such a practice is similar to the first stage in *lectio divina*, as described by a twelfth-century Carthusian monk called Guigo. He described the stages he saw as essential to the practice, the first of which is *lectio* itself (reading), in which the monk reads a passage from the Word of God slowly and reflectively so that it sinks into both mind and heart.

As Fr. Michael Patella points out in *Word and Image: The Hermeneutics of the Saint John's Bible*, the practice of *lectio divina* also inspires the free skills of an educated person:

> In the practice of *lectio divina*, human experience both meets and
> is interpreted through the biblical text. It is not so much a process
> that filters out thoughts and experiences that seemingly have no
> biblical context, inasmuch as these same thoughts and experiences
> are converted into a scriptural idiom with biblical references. For
> example, personal struggles are tied to biblical figures and events,
> daily ambiguities are cast into the ambit of the mystery of God,
> and human love is seen within the realm of divine love. There is
> no end to what can be interpreted through the scriptural tradition.
> No thought is considered unworthy or profane, for even tangents
> of thought are under the Holy Spirit.[2]

This is not to say that *lectio divina* is an anti-intellectual practice; scholarly
research into a particular text as well as the contributions of the arts and
sciences to an understanding of scripture are equally important. But according to Fr. Patella, while "the ancient fourfold model of exegesis—literal,
allegorical, moral and anagogical, in which the literal level establishes the
normative text and the allegorical opens up to the normative meanings of
the text," was used by the CIT in developing the Saint John's Bible, this
model was not exhaustive. Rather, "the term allegorical moves well beyond
its original meaning now to include intra- and intertextuality."[3] Likewise,
Great Books students learned to make use of the mass of scholarly notes
that accompany the works of Dante and Milton to establish literal, allegorical, intra- and intertextual meanings of each text.

To challenge the painting students to move beyond stereotypical images of Dante and Milton's works, Professor Batcheller directed the student painters to develop a more modern intertextual relationship with the
Inferno and *Paradise Lost* by creating a collage of images gleaned from
contemporary magazines. Milton and Dante's narratives are disruptive
of student's notions of sin, divine justice, Eve, Satan, and paradise. Such
disruption engenders the second stage of *lectio*, which is *meditatio* (reflection) where one thinks about the text one has chosen and ruminates
upon it so that one takes from it what God wants to give. The language of
each poem beckons the reader to imagine scenes of sin, damnation, and
paradise afresh, and, in either a written brief or a collage, to merge the
language of the poem with the language of design. Such a move is akin
to the third stage of *lectio*, known as *oratio* (response), which is inspired
by one's reflection on the Word of God. In this way, scholarly references,

2. Patella, *Word and Image*, 15.
3. Ibid., 323.

personal experience with the text, and images drawn from the reader's imagination and contemporary culture come together in a hermeneutic that is truly incarnational. Whether or not the literal, allegorical and moral aspects of Dante and Milton give rise to the anagogical (or life in Christ) is up to the individual students and the viewers of the paintings. At the very least, however, the inter-textual milieu of *lectio divina,* and the model of exegesis employed—in which one is encouraged to use all the tools at one's disposal—serves as an inexhaustible source of inspiration for creating a collaborative learning environment.

Practical Details

Because we sought to create a sacred learning environment and not merely a "Maker's Space" or "Fab Lab," we worked carefully to develop prompts and guidelines for the collaboration, which are explained in more detail below. Nevertheless, our message to the students was consistent: collaboration is a messy process, a meeting at the crossroads that requires listening to the text, communication, problem solving and a constant reframing of ideas in order to be successful.

The project began on the Great Books side of the collaboration. After reading the texts and engaging in shared inquiry in seminar, Professor Rodeheffer led a discussion in which students nominated scenes whose language conjured images that were especially redolent of important themes from the text, and which thus made them especially conducive to illustration. The Great Books students then worked together in small groups to isolate textual passages in Dante's *Inferno* or Milton's *Paradise Lost* that could serve as the narrative basis for a work of art. This approach follows that of the Committee on Illumination and Text in choosing biblical texts for visual interpretation in *The Saint John's Bible*. As Fr. Patella writes, "Some texts are more complex than others, and while all were chosen to correspond to the framework of the project plan, there are biblical passages that have greater resonance in doing so."[4] The students took to this task with significant enthusiasm, and at the end of the class period individual students were tasked with writing a three-page brief in which they presented a vision of the scene their group had isolated, based on their own textual analysis. The prompt follows below.

4. Ibid., 75.

Divining Milton Prompt

In collaboration with Professor Batcheller's Drawing Course, we will be working with students to inspire drawings of scenes from Milton's *Paradise Lost*. Before meeting with the drawing students the week of October 12th, each of you needs to prepare a brief for the section you have chosen to work on. The statement should be 2 ¾ to 3 pages in length and should include:

1. a brief discussion of the characters involved and the action taking place in the passage,

2. the mood Milton is trying to convey (fear, delight, anger, disdain, etc.), and

3. a discussion of which words you see as most important. ("When Milton says 'squat like a toad,' I imagine . . ." or, "When Milton says the waters of the Lake Eve looks into are 'Pure as the expanse of Heaven,' I imagine the lake as . . .")

Use descriptive adjectives to paint a picture of the scene in words, with as many details as you can imagine—even facial expressions. Communicate what the focal point should be, i.e. the dominant element that you want to draw the viewer's attention to.

The following website provides descriptions of the basic elements of design. After discussing the focal point, pick three or four other design elements and give the artist some direction. I would suggest choosing from among shape, color, value, texture, balance and proportion, but look at the definitions and see what fits with your vision for the scene. The essay should have a brief introduction but don't worry about a conclusion. You will be adding 2–3 more pages about viewing the work of art after the drawing is completed.

http://flyeschool.com/content/elements-artdesign -and-principles-designorganization

In evaluating the vision statement, I will be looking at the degree to which you convey your insights into Milton's language in rich, visual language. Stay close to the text, and draw on the notes as needed to understand the context.

The scenes are listed below:

Paradise Lost Scenes

A. Sin being born out of Satan's Head: Book 2

You will need to draw on language describing Sin from several places. Begin with the bottom of p. 66 to top of p. 67, just after the Furies have threatened Satan and Sin rises to speak to him. Ll. 723–26 "had not the snaky sorceress . . ." Also look at Stan's reaction upon seeing Sin for the first time and her description of her birth, pp. 67–8, ll. 741–67. "What thing thou art . . ." to "A growing burden . . . ." If any of the language about Sin giving birth to Death helps you to imagine her, draw on that as well (ll. 777–808). You will need to decide if you want to imagine her just being born or pregnant with Death.

B. Eve viewing her reflection in the Lake: Book 4

P. 125, ll. 449–69 ("That day I oft remember . . ." to "With thee it came and goes . . .") To get a sense of what Eve looks like, see Book 4, ll. 288–324, "Two of far nobler shape," to "the fairest of her daughters, Eve."

C. "Squat Like a Toad": Book 4

Pp. 136–7, ll. 797–822 ("So saying, on he led . . ." to "unmoved with fear, accost him soon.") To imagine Satan, you may wish to draw on language that describes the various looks on his face as he figures out how to gain entrance to Paradise: Book 4, p. 112, ll. 115–30 ("Thus while he spake . . ." to "all unobserved, unseen.")

D. Satan Leaps over the Walls of Paradise: Book 4

You will need to draw on language that describe the various looks on Satan's face as he figures out how to gain entrance to Paradise: p. 112, ll. 115–130 ("Thus while he spake . . ." to "all unobserved, unseen.") The wall itself is described on pp. 113–4, ll. 132–59 ("of Eden, where delicious Paradise" to "Those balmy spoils.") Satan actually climbs the wall beginning on p. 115, ll. 172–92, ("Now to the ascent" to "this first grand thief into God's fold.")

E. "Then Satan First Knew Pain": Book 6

The scene is set on p. 181, ll. 56–73. If you want to include Satan's chariot, it is described on pp. 182–3, ll. 99–110. Abdiel Lifting his sword against Satan: p. 185–6, ll. 189–200. The archangel Michael is described on p. 187, beginning on l. 246, "till Satan, who that

Day" and ending on the top of p. 188, "a vast circumference." The actual battle takes place on p. 189–90, beginning with l. 296, "They ended parle" and ending at l. 343, "equal God in power." To imagine Satan, you may wish to draw on language that describes the various looks on his face as he figures out how to gain entrance to Paradise: Book 4, p. 112, ll. 115–30 ("Thus while he spake . . . to "all unobserved, unseen.") Revisit other passages where Satan is described in his armor (e.g., Book 1, pp. 18–19, ll. 283–300, and pp. 31–2, ll. 588–606. Look for other passages as well!!!)

Once the briefs were completed, the collaboration moved to phase two, in which each art student read the briefs for her particular scene, and, sketch book in hand, met with the small group of Great Books students to flesh out a vision for the work of art. The art students were then tasked with using their expertise in the aesthetic components of the mediums of painting or multimedia to translate the information into a visual context. Over the course of the collaboration we found that a ratio of two or three Great Books students to one Art student was ideal; too much input can strain the ability of the artist to develop a coherent vision.

As Professor Rodeheffer was asking students to stretch their skills of textual analysis into a visual context, Professor Batcheller sought to coax her art students into spaces where they could ask questions that go beyond the exploration of subject and form—i.e. beyond issues of whether or not the color palette is correct, the paint is applied correctly, and the forms being painted are proportionate. In addition to these basic elements of subject and form, the art students were directed to focus on *content*, which requires a more nuanced visual acuity. Such acuity is developed through attention to the principles and elements of design and the way in which specific tools and materials can be used to arrange objects on a canvas. The marriage of subject and form with content is usually a struggle for art students at this level, and Professor Batcheller has found that this goal is most successfully reached if she asks her students to convey a story or narrative. The Great Books students fulfilled that role in providing a narrative drawn from the *Inferno* or *Paradise Lost*, which aided considerably in this process of conceptual growth. Professor Batcheller likens this process to Jacob wrestling with the angel. To this end, she presented the painting students with a list of guidelines. As mentioned above, for the first time in the semester, they were invited to use a full color palette and they were directed to create a collage of the text they were illustrating from brightly saturated magazine images that represented the full color spectrum. This collage then served as source material from which to paint.

The painting students were also directed to make use of the other essential elements of design (line, shape, value and texture), with one limitation: the only tool they could use to apply the paint was a palette knife. By using only a palette knife, students were forced to consider texture and paint application differently than if they were using a paintbrush. The paint application becomes thicker and enhances the ability of the artist to create a variety of physical textures on the canvas. In addition, the awkwardness of using a palette knife empowers rigid painters to loosen up and discover new painting styles. The project thus followed the natural trajectory of artistic research, in which broader concepts are gradually distilled into finer distinctions. In the collaboration between the two courses, the original directive to collaborate was reframed and refined over a period of several meetings between the two groups of students, which resulted in either an oil painting or a multimedia work.

In the intermediate drawing course, Professor Batcheller introduced the students to a new material called Yupo, which is a waterproof, synthetic, tree-free paper. It offers a unique alternative to traditional paper and is an excellent surface for water-based media such as ink, watercolor, and acrylic paints. In this particular project, the challenge for intermediate students was greater: they did not have a collage to work from, and with no imagery in front of them they were required to pull the design from the briefs of the Great Books students and their own imagination. What they were learning in terms of materials was thus coupled with the task of figuring out their visual voice in the context of *Paradise Lost*. This experimentation pushed the art students to move beyond overused stereotypes and helped those whose creativity had become stagnant to produce more resonant works of art.

Once the art works were completed, the Great Books students wrote a second piece in which they responded to the artwork in three parts. This second prompt asked them to reflect on the following questions:

  a. In viewing the artwork, what do you see first? Do you think this is what the artist wants you to see first?

  b. Why did you see it first? Does it have a bright color, is it in the center of the piece, does it have a texture that is different from the rest of the piece, is it an awkward moment in the piece?

  c. What path does your eye follow through the work?

  d. Are there any places where your eye gets stuck? Why?

  e. What interests you the most about this piece? Why?

In Part II, students were asked to transition to their experience the Artist's Muse:

  a. What aspects of your discussion with and suggestions to the artist are reflected in the final painting? Does the artist's rendering evoke the central themes, mood, activity, or characters of your assigned scene? What part of the scene from the *Inferno* or *Paradise Lost* has the artist chosen to highlight?

b. What line or lines from the *Inferno* or *Paradise Lost* does the painting best illustrate? Quote at least two passages.

c. What do you question about the artist's interpretation of the *Inferno* or *Paradise Lost*? Why?

d. What would be an appropriate title for this piece?

Finally, in Part III the students were asked to write a brief conclusion in which they stated their reasons for determining whether or not the collaboration was a successful one.

Upon completion of their responses to the artwork, the Great Books students joined the Art students in the painting or drawing studio for a formal critique of the artwork. Critique is a necessary component of the creative process, especially for young artists. It provides a forum for the artist to see areas in need of improvement through input from their peers, and to consider whether or not the audience perceives the intended meaning of the artwork. Professor Batcheller invited the Great Books students to join the Art students in asking and answering questions and exploring details of the works the original briefs had inspired. The collaboration culminated in a pop-up exhibition in the Payson Gallery at Pepperdine University in the spring of 2014. In this final stage of implementation, the Painters and their Muses were invited to discuss the project with audience members who visited the gallery. The art works and selections from the briefs and responses to the artworks were also featured in our undergraduate Great Books journal, *Athena's Gate*. Through this collaboration, humanities and art students entered into a centuries old tradition of interpreting and illustrating the *Inferno* and *Paradise Lost*.

Musing Dante

In what follows we will provide brief discussions of four paintings that were completed in the *Musing Dante* project from the perspective of the painter's conceptual and artistic growth, followed by selections from the briefs by Great Books students based on textual passages from the *Inferno*; these were translated into collages, which formed the template for oil paintings of the Gates of Dis in Canto IX of the *Inferno* and the Fraudulent in the *Malebolge*, those evil ditches of the eighth Circle of Hell.

This artist was able to draw out very fine details using only a palette knife to produce a realistic rendering of Dante's description of Phlegethon, the river of blood into which those who shed the blood of their neighbors are sent to boil in Cantos XII-XIII of the *Inferno*.

This painting is more abstract than the River of Blood image; nevertheless it is still somewhat representational of the giant Antaeus lifting Dante and Virgil in his hand and placing them in the 9th circle of Hell. The palette knife allowed the artist to utilize a consistently rough texture across the surface.

In her response to the above painting of the Heavenly Messenger arriving to scatter the furies and open the gates of Hell, a Great Books student wrote the following: "During my discussion with the artist, I mentioned that Virgil and Dante should be differentiated from each other because Dante is living and Virgil is not—he is a shade. The way the artist interprets this difference from Virgil is very astute in that Virgil is depicted as a large, ambiguous figure and Dante as the crave-ridden she-wolf who haunts the pilgrim in the dark wood. I found it particularly clever of the artist to liken the heavenly messenger to a professional hurdler who overcomes obstacles. Dante writes that the heavenly messenger who comes to disperse Medusa and the Furies prior to unlocking the Gates of Dis appears 'full of high disdain.' The painter captures this language in the image of a professional hurdler who must tilt her face upward to clear each bar."

Another student focused on the artist's depiction of the Furies as beach-going sorority girls: "In Virgil's classical world, the Furies appear as a gruesome and terrifying trio: the 'daughters of Night' marked by blood-stained faces and snakes twirling in their hair and about their waists. They symbolized obstinacy and pride and were often invoked by offended mortals and gods to exact revenge. In a biting reference to Pepperdine's Greek life culture, the painter depicts the Furies as sorority girls basking on the beach, the coiled snake suggesting they are completely embroiled in the latest mean girls gossip." In her depiction of the heavenly messenger as a high hurdler and the Furies as sorority girls, the painter follows the example of the CIT in drawing on images rooted in a particular place and time. In his discussion of the ways in which art and text overlap in *The Saint John's Bible* to "draw in, as much as possible, a full sensory reading of the bible," Fr. Michael Patella relies on Robin M. Jensen's *The Substance of Things Seen: Art, Faith and the Christian Community*. While any given image should never be a viewer's sole or total experience with the text,

> Art that is didactic must do more that relay information as a literalistic rendering of the story; it must also impart "a point of view, dimension, and amplification of the narrative." Art that is prophetic cannot become propaganda; its goal must be to "call forth personal transformation, not to sell as particular product or idea."[5]

In provoking viewers by imparting a particular view of sorority culture in light of Medusa and her Furies, the painting is both didactic and prophetic.

5. Ibid., 18, 20.

In his directions to the artist assigned to the punishment of the fraud-ulent, a Great Books student wrote, "Dante describes this sight of the ser-pents as 'cruel' and 'depressing.' I would depict the snakes as very large and intimidating with many coils and a flared neck to make them look more threatening. They should have their double-pointed tongues sticking out; this feature should be exaggerated in the snakes to symbolize the double-personality of a thief, who must deceitfully fool his victims while appearing kind and just on the outside. Among the snakes are naked and terrified people running around hopelessly, with no place to hide. Their hands are tied behind their backs by the serpents. The serpents 'thrust their head and tail right through the loins' (XXIV, l. 95), and twist themselves around the other side. The *contrapasso* (a punishment that is a fitting reflection of the sin) wrought by the snakes in this pouch of Hell should be central to the painting since snakes are deceitful and stealthy, just like thieves."

Divining Milton

Based on our experience with *Musing Dante*, we transitioned the collabo-ration to intermediate art students and students in the final Great Books course. We called this collaboration *Divining Milton*, and it was completed in the fall of 2015. To enhance the essays produced by the Great Books students, Professor Rodeheffer included a discussion of the principles and elements of Design in her prompt and directed students to employ this terminology in both their briefs for the artists and their responses to the completed paintings. Professor Batcheller directed her drawing students to use a variety of drawing and painting media in an exploratory process using the synthetic drawing surface Yupo.

In his brief, a Great Books student pointed out the following: "Sin's birth is rooted in the ancient myth of Athena's genesis. Just as Athena was born out of Zeus's head, so Sin is begotten from the head of Satan. Eve says to Satan, 'All of a sudden, miserable pain surprised thee, dim thine eyes, and dizzy swum in darkness, while thy head flames thick and fast threw forth, till on the left side opening wide, likest to thee in shape and countenance bright, then shining heavenly fair, a goddess armed out of thy head I sprung?' (2.751–56). Certain themes and words jump off the page in that passage. Milton's tone is one of horror and repulsion, so I imagine Sin's emergence from Satan's mind to be horrific, sickening, and gruesome as well. The flames literally eat through his false exterior, revealing the true soul within and creating a portal through which Sin aggressively 'springs' forth. She splits '[open] wide' the left side of his skull and claws her way out (2.755). Sin is described by Milton as a 'snaky sorceress' (2.724), seeming like a 'woman to the waist and fair, but [ending] foul in many a scaly fold, voluminous and vast, a serpent armed with mortal sting' (2.650–52). I imagine Sin to appear like an unnatural extension of Satan's brain, violently piercing through flesh, a nauseating evil that was never meant to see daylight. As his skull rips open, the terribly beautiful woman greedily and hastily crawls out, her eyes hungry, her snakelike lower-half one with the innards of Satan's mind, 'scaly folds' merging with the folds of his brain, a scorpion-like tail ('mortal sting') raised behind her. This juxtaposition of beautiful and fair with scaly and foul could make for the most interesting contrast in the scene. Sin could even be portrayed as two characters here to emphasize the contrast and deviousness of her nature. This is the birth of something that should not be, a hopelessly sad mutilation of creation."

In her description of Eve coming upon her image reflected in a lake, another Great Books student directed the artist to focus on the water: "When Milton describes Eve hearing a 'murmuring sound of water . . . spread into a liquid plain, then stood unmoved pure as the expanse of Heaven' (4:451–54), I imagine the water to be a crystal blue that has a glass-like texture to it, translucent and pure. The water should appear as if it is real water, almost inviting the viewer to reach out and touch the surface. In rendering the water as shaded like glass the artist will echo Milton's idea that the water in the lake is ultimately a mirror reflecting both the image of Eve and the image of God through his creation. Milton describes Eve approaching the calm lake, as a 'clear smooth lake that to [her] seemed another sky' (4:458–59). In terms of color and texture, the drawing should

173

suggest the color of heaven as reflected in Paradise. In regards to value, I see the lake as bright and light, with the value slowly getting darker farther away from the lake. The surrounding flowers and plants should be richer and rendered in various colors. Overall, I want the feeling of the scene to be one that calms and delights, based on Eve's response to seeing her image, 'I started Back, It started back' (4:462–63). I want the presence of the lake to be a peaceful focal point, while there may be some hints of darkness upon further examination."

We engaged in a third collaboration involving the *Oresteia*, a set of three Greek tragedies by Aeschylus in the fall of 2016. In the coming years we plan to sustain this project through further collaborations involving Homer's *Odyssey* and Dostoevsky's *The Brothers Karamazov*. We are hopeful that these ongoing projects will continue to open our students to the liberal arts as a transformative experience in which collaborating across disciplinary fields provokes new insights into classical texts, enhances visual literacy, and contributes to the conceptual and artistic skills of artists in training. Our ultimate objective as teachers and mentors is to facilitate this journey, whereby students realize their potential, as evolving artists and intellectuals, to engage in the sacramental experience of relating text to image, thereby ensuring their role as both debtors and stewards of the *artes liberales* tradition.

Bibliography

Alighieri, Dante. *The Divine Comedy*. Translated by Allen Mandelbaum. New York: Penguin Random House, 1995.

Jensen, Robin M. *The Substance of Things Seen: Art, Faith and the Christian Community*. Grand Rapids: Eerdmans, 2004.

Kimball, Bruce A. *Orators and Philosophers: A History of the Idea of Liberal Education*. New York: College Board, 1995.

Milton, John. *Paradise Lost*. Ed. David Scott Kastan. Indianapolis: Hackett, 2005.

Patella, Michael. *Word and Image: The Hermeneutics of the Saint John's Bible*. Collegeville, MN: Liturgical, 2013.

Index

Scripture Index